The 2010s

Looking Back at a Dramatic Decade

By Jason Strong

Copyright

Contents

Introduction

The 2010s. Was it a time of prosperity and technological advancement or a decade lost to internet memes, distracting social media and "fake news"? There is no doubt the 2010s was an eventful period, with some of the highest highs and the lowest lows of the current young millennia. We emerged from the 2000s a hardy bunch, having endured distressing events including 9/11, natural disasters like hurricane Katrina and the 2008 economic downturn, which caused global financial turmoil. Yet the 2000s also witnessed many landmark achievements, notably the election of America's first black president whose work earned him a Nobel Peace Prize and the rise of a ubiquitous internet. The majority of countries witnessed a general shift to more accepting societies, improving the quality of life for millions of people around the world.

Many departed the "noughties," believing the worst was behind us. Unfortunately, the 2010s did not have the best start either. Whilst still suffering from the infamous 2007 global recession, the 2010s started amidst low-interest rates, stagnant wages, a housing crisis in most of the U.S., and a sovereign debt crisis in much of Europe. Unfortunate events increased throughout the rest of the decade. In 2014, the mysterious disappearance of a Malaysia Airlines passenger jet devastated the world. The whereabouts of the 239 passengers and crew on-board are still unknown— making it one of the biggest aviation mysteries in history. Treasonous crimes were committed in Syria, where chemical gas was administered on its own civilians by the tyrannical Syrian government. Elsewhere in the world, technology has become so sophisticated many workers fear for their jobs.

Yet, it was not all doom and gloom. Modern medical advances have gifted the world with better control over health epidemics. Since 2010, global HIV/AIDS infection rates have fallen by 16% in adults and by 35% for children. Tanzania revealed that in the last ten years, it had reduced the malaria death rate by 50% in adults and 53% in children. Many countries are now on track to eliminate third-world diseases completely by 2030.

There has also been much advancement in global peace efforts. Ethiopia and Eritrea signed a peace treaty, signaling the end of a 20-year war and reuniting thousands of families. In 2018, the world surpassed the four million mark for electric vehicles, signifying a long-overdue departure from decades of over-reliance on fossil fuels.

Aside from the good and the bad, we also had the downright peculiar. Social media trends such as planking, the "Harlem Shake," and the ice bucket challenge took the world by storm. The augmented reality game, Pokémon Go, had both children and adults around the world chasing virtual monsters throughout the streets. In film and media, Leonardo DiCaprio finally won his first Oscar.

This review aims to explore the most significant events of the past 10 years, both positive and negative, to make sense of the second decade of the millennia. The most important events, spanning across politics, business, science, technology, and culture, will all be explored to reveal many trends and surprises you may not have realized. In doing so, we can seek lessons to be learned before entering the 2020s. As

William Wordsworth once quipped: "Life is divided into three terms
- that which was, which is, and which will be. Let us learn from the
past to profit by the present, and from the present, to live better in
the future".

1. Politics

United States vs. China

Clash of the Titans

"America at this moment," said the former British Prime Minister Winston Churchill in 1945 "stands at the summit of the world." During the 1950s, it was easy to see what Churchill meant. The United States was the world's strongest military power. Its economy was booming, and the fruits of this prosperity were evident; the streets were filled with new Cadillacs and Corvettes, and large suburban houses. New leisure activities and economic gave Americans what the rest of the world could only dream of. Since then, the U.S.A has ruled the world order seemingly unchallenged.

All good things must come to an end, however, as the past decade has witnessed a significant shift in the global power hierarchy. Whilst the U.S., having emerged from World War II as the dominant player in global politics, has maintained its position as the authoritative figure in world politics for the past 70 years, the last 10 of those have revealed the emergence of serious cracks in America's political hegemony. The balance of power now looks set to shift to other countries for good. Whilst these cracks have been forming out of site for quite some time, recent U.S.-centric political policies by President Donald Trump have forced these issues to the surface, revealing the ugly truth no American wants to hear – that America's top position as a global superpower is slowly fading.

The reasons for America's loss of global influence are numerous and diverse. In the 1950s, having just recovered their industry from the damage of the war, the U.S. produced roughly half of all global economic output. It held this position well into the 1990s, wherein the collapse of the Soviet Union removed the only tangible threat to U.S. dominance. The U.S. military ruled the seas and was capable of deploying both defensive and offensive forces almost anywhere in the world, gifting America, with the ultimate leverage in any negotiation. America currently manages to sustain this longstanding position of power, but the gap is closing against rising powers such as Russia and China.

America's most powerful weapon in securing global power does not lie in its military forces, however. The U.S. dollar is by far the most powerful weapon in its arsenal. The greenback has been the global currency (or reserve currency) for quite some time. As of 2018, 62% of all known central bank foreign currency reserves (money or other assets held by a central bank or other monetary authority so that it can pay its liabilities if needed) are held in U.S. dollars, making it the unofficial de facto global currency. The U.S. dollar has managed to hold such great influence for so long due to the continued strength of the U.S. economy, instilling confidence that storing wealth in U.S. dollars is among the safest way to store currency. This is particularly vital in foreign countries with volatile currencies, such as Venezuela, where inflation rose to over 1,000,000% at its worst. With the Venezuelan Bolivar rendered essentially useless, the U.S. dollar became the new unofficial currency. As a result, close to 30% of all transactions in Venezuela are now denominated in U.S. dollars. This is a familiar occurrence elsewhere in the world. As a result, almost 65% of all dollar bills are held outside the U.S., symbolizing the global dominance of the U.S. greenback today. The U.S. mortgage crisis of 2007 originated as a local issue within the country. Still, the far-reaching influence of the dollar quickly spread to the rest of the world, creating an unprecedented global economic recession which we are still yet to fully recover from.

The U.S. dollar's dominance may have reached its peak, however. With new protectionist regulations introduced through President Donald Trump's "America First" policy, many former trading partners now realize how an overreliance on the U.S. dollar is exposing them to great risk and leaving them at the mercy of unpredictable American policies. Countries are fervently turning to other currencies in a bid to hedge their financial positions. In response to the controversial U.S. sanctions imposed on Iran – against the better judgment of U.S. allies – European Union (EU) diplomats are planning to set up a "special purpose vehicle" that would allow European countries to skirt U.S. sanctions on Iran through a new payment vehicle that doesn't involve dollars.

Political events such as these are encouraging the president of the European Commission, Jean-Claude Juncker, to initiate a long-term shift away from the U.S. dollar towards other strong currencies. One of the main contenders is the Euro. "The Euro must become the face, the instrument of a new, more sovereign Europe," he said. In spite of his noble efforts, the Euro has yet to reach the benchmarks previously determined by the U.S. dollar. Amid a sovereign debt crisis in Europe, the past decade has seen the territory's share in currency reserves fall from 26% to 20%. It is still too early to judge the capacity of the Euro; however – as compared to the 70-year-old Dollar, the former has only existed for the past two decades.

Furthermore, there's China. China's growth and global influence over the past decade has been both unforeseen and unparalleled. Its emergence as a new superpower to rival that of the U.S. has boosted confidence in its own currency, the Renminbi, which is increasing at a time when the U.S. dollar is beginning to wane. Whilst the dollar still dominates today, the latest data from the International Monetary Fund (IMF) shows that its popularity is slipping. In the second quarter of 2018, 62.3% of the world's $10.5 trillion in allocated reserves were denominated in U.S. dollars, the smallest share since 2013. This is a decrease from 62.5% in the previous quarter and 63.8% the year before. Admittedly, the decreases are small, but they do continue a long gradual trend of decline since its peak of 73% in 2001.

So, the dollar is weakening, and the euro is nowhere near strong enough to replace it. What about the Chinese renminbi? Since November 2015, the IMF awarded the Chinese currency the coveted status as a reserve currency, meaning that central banks can now hold the renminbi in its stores, joining the U.S. dollar, Euro, Dutch guilder, pound sterling, Japanese yen, Swiss franc, and Canadian dollar as the basket of internationally recognized safe currencies. As much promise as the renminbi – and by extension China – shows as a dominant economic powerhouse, the renminbi is unlikely to surpass the U.S. dollar for one fundamental reason: the lack of confidence in China's economy. China, while moving towards the ideals of capitalism, is still very much a highly restricted market that is controlled by the authoritarian Chinese national party with an iron fist, which is a stark contrast to the free-market approach that the U.S. is highly prized for. This high level of state control in China leaves the largest Asian market susceptible to state manipulation, which significantly reduces investor confidence in its reliability. For the renminbi to surpass the dollar, China needs to become an accountable democracy and build a track record of abiding by international laws, along with transforming their economic landscape with open stock markets and full accountability. It appears that under the autocratic rule of President Xi Jinping, this isn't going to happen anytime soon.

There still remains the question of who will fill this global power void if confidence in the U.S. dollar continues to fall, and potential successors, such as the euro and renminbi, are still too weak to take over. The answer may be unexpected and even be considered a trick question. The most likely answer is there simply won't be a single dominant currency. The past half-century has seen the U.S. dollar singlehandedly dominate global financial markets, but this has not always been the case. For example, in the period between the two world wars, the British pound and U.S. dollar shared reserve currency status almost equally. Even before this, the French franc and German marc were also equally significant.

Looking back to past economic times, which reveals that this current period of single currency dominance is the anomaly, where the unusual absence of competitor currencies has allowed the dollar to monopolize the international currency role. History also suggests that the dollar's time as the single dominant currency is not sustainable, and global markets will eventually return to their natural equilibrium where multiple currencies can successfully coexist. Current trajectories suggest that the U.S. dollar, euro, and yuan will share prominence. Yet, the time frame in which this could occur remains uncertain and highly dependent on the actions of Xi Jinping and Donald Trump. This may not be a bad thing, however. If the ultimate goal is to secure a safer and more stable economy, this may well rest on a financial system that relies on three pillars - the dollar, the euro and the renminbi.

The Rise of China

Rise and Shine

Many have likened China to the Chinese dragon – a symbol of imperial strength and power – which has been hibernating out of sight for the past 50 years. From a record 32% share of the global GDP in 1820 - when the Qing dynasty emperor Daoguang began his reign – China hit rock bottom at the end of the Cultural Revolution in 1976 with a share of just 5% when almost two-thirds of the Chinese population lived in dire poverty.

And yet, by 2019, China's share of global GDP had climbed to nearly 19%. This past decade has seen the emergence of a new superpower, which previous U.S. President Barack Obama first recognized during a meeting with then Chinese President Hu Jintao in 2011. The current trade wars between the U.S. and China are a manifestation of the relatively sudden realization that China is now very much on a path to establish themselves as an economic powerhouse, which has the very real potential to unseat America as the most influential power.

China's political ascendancy took American Politicians by surprise, having orchestrated its incredible rise from a position of relative weakness. Nobody in the West expected a socialist regime to produce any real progress which would be capable of competing with democratic norms, especially after the collapse of the then most powerful socialist state, the Soviet Union (USSR). Socialism was always linked to failure and democracy to success, with many declaring that China would eventually go the way of the other "Asian Tigers" - Japan, Taiwan, and South Korea – and embrace democracy as they grew richer. Yet China bucked this trend and has used its authoritarian single-party power to forcibly mold the economy to its own agenda.

China is not any old socialist regime, however. The economic reform that started in China in 1978 under the guidance of the previous chief leader, Deng Xiaoping, was termed "socialism with Chinese characteristics." This special take on socialism aims to benefit from the best of both worlds by using capitalist free-market economics to foster economic growth whilst retaining its formal commitment to communism and conserving its authoritative political power. This setup has allowed China to create an excellent environment for economic growth without having to answer to constitutional laws that restrict Western countries (to the benefit of its citizens).

After 30 years of this "socialism with Chinese characteristics," the change and growth in China and its economy has been profound. According to official statistics, economic growth has averaged 9.5% over the past two decades compared to America's 2.71%, with national income doubling on average every eight years. Such an increase in output represents one of the most sustained and rapid economic transformations throughout the world's economy in the last half-century. Figure 1 compares real GDP growth for both China and the U.S. over the past 40 years.

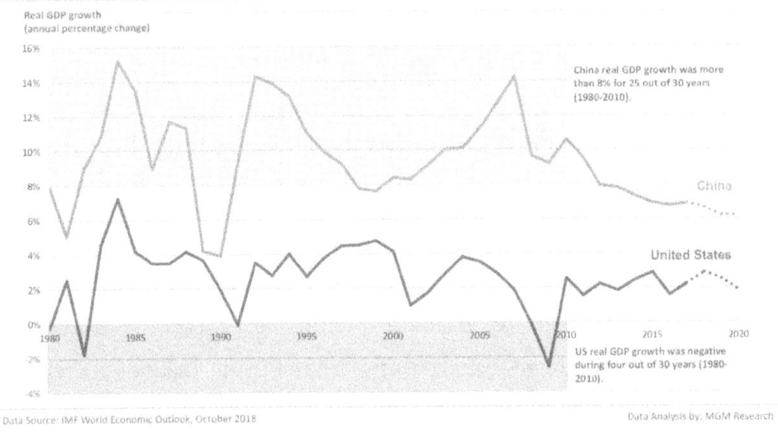

Figure 1: Real GDP growth U.S. vs. China over 40 years.

It is not just economic might that has seen China's stature rise. China has overtaken the U.S. as the world's largest trading nation having been the largest exporter of goods since 2009. The Asian nation has also filed the most patents, expanded its military powers, supervised the landing of lunar rovers on the moon as well as creating a major film and cultural center. The publication of scientific articles in China grew by 23.4% per year in the decade to 2008, the fastest in the world for that period. The past decade has seen a continuation in this trend, with China nurturing its own homegrown source of intellectual wealth that it previously had to acquire from abroad. China has also developed its own foreign policy through such schemes as the controversial "Belt and Road Initiative", an ambitious program aiming to connect Asia with Africa and Europe via new land and maritime networks. Despite this admirable drive for success, the way in which China conducts these initiatives has been ethically questionable. The Belt and Road initiative has often been accused of trapping poorer nations with lures of cheap loans and unrealistic repayment schedules in order to exert influence in these regions when they inevitably fail to repay these dubious loans.

Since the 2008 collapse of the investment bank Lehman Brothers and the ensuing global financial crisis, China's leaders have been deeply worried about just how susceptible to U.S. economics China really is. This was no better demonstrated than in October 2008 when its stock market spectacularly crashed from a high of 6,124 in 2007 to 1,664 in 2008, a record-breaking fall that China has yet to recover from. Events like these convinced Chinese policy makers that a shift away from exports and growth of domestic consumption was needed in order to reduce their susceptibility from foreign dependents, particularly the U.S.

This long-term effort to reduce China's exposure to U.S. politics now appears to be paying dividends. The past decade has seen the birth of a whole new Chinese middle class, raising millions out of poverty and reducing the numbers of those who were restricted to unfruitful farming in rural areas as one of the only sources of income. China's middle class has now expanded to 200-300 million strong and continues to grow rapidly. The country's new strategic imperatives have shifted to reducing debt risk, boosting aggregate demand and deploying massive economic stimulus to encourage domestic consumption, all with the aim of decreasing China's vulnerability to external economic shocks.

With increasing economic productivity comes a need for better infrastructure. And nowhere in the world has the development of infrastructure been as rapid or extensive as China. China has invested in nearly 30,000km of high-speed rail frameworks, resulting in a railway network capable of transporting over 3 billion people a year. Improvements in infrastructure has also increased urbanization, facilitated closer regional ties and enhanced consumption considerably.

As a result, China's economy almost tripled in size between 2008-2018 with its GDP reaching 90 trillion yuan (U.S. $3.6 trillion). China became the new dominant "Asian Tiger", having grown from half the size of Japan's GDP in 2008 to over 2.3 times in 2016.

Compared to the U.S.'s tech hub in Silicon Valley which has dominated technology developments and investments for over 100 years, China's rise in technological prowess has emerged only relatively recently. Behemoth Chinese tech companies such as Alibaba, Tencent and Baidu rank as the 6th, 7th and 13th largest corporations in the world, rapidly catching the U.S. tech giants in terms of revenue. In fact, nine of the 20 largest global tech companies are now Chinese. However, cynics have accused China of reaching this level through unfair practices, most notably by stealing foreign intellectual property (IP), especially that of American IP. Intellectual property theft has been a longstanding issue that has ramped up in intensity this past decade, culminating in the current trade war between the US and China with $250 billion worth of tariffs on Chinese imports and $325 billion more threatened. No matter what your opinion of President Trump may be, his defense of American IP is an issue which has been long coming.

A CNBC poll found that one in five U.S. corporations believe that China has stolen intellectual property from them in the past year, including intangible valuables such as patents, trade secrets, trademarks and copyrights. The theft of intangible assets may seem trivial as no direct value has been taken, but the indirect costs are very severe. Intangible assets, which include IP, make up 80% of the S&P 500 companies' value, according to the Harvard business review. Whilst the damage to business from theft of intangibles is not immediately apparent, it represents either a future loss of opportunity or a loss in competitive advantage, reducing the profit earned from an initial investment. The U.S. trade representative now estimates current annual losses of IP between $225 - $600 billion to China alone.

Stealing IP is usually difficult, but China now seems to have mastered the craft. Corporate espionage and cyberattacks are two common ways which IP is often stolen, as the traces are often faint, and evidence of tampering is difficult to prove. What is perhaps more worrying, however, are forced technology transfers in which the Chinese government compels companies investing in China to provide sensitive IP details and licenses in exchange for access to its rapidly expanding and lucrative markets. Many foreign businesses deem this a price to pay a piece of the large China pie, but it could be considered a form of financial extortion.

There is also strong evidence suggesting that China has used foreign-ownership restrictions to pressure American companies into using local technology firms as opposed to bringing in their home technologies, which leads to American firms often giving up control to unreliable Chinese companies with dubious regulations, laws and agendas. Although an accurate number is difficult to calculate, a 2015 paper by the Federal Reserve Bank of Minneapolis concluded that more than half of all technology owned by Chinese firms was obtained from foreign companies.

The problem is so prominent and damaging even the Chinese have recognized it as a problem. Fearing a potential drop in foreign investment as espionage and theft complaints scare newcomers away, Chinese President Xi Jinping highlighted, in a speech dating as far back as 2017, the need to speed up IP protection and called for stricter enforcement where any infringer must pay a "heavy price." In December of the same year, China announced its most serious measures since the trade war erupted, including punishments that could restrict local companies' access to borrowing and state-funding should they engage in IP theft. The government said in the following January that it would accelerate the passage of a new foreign-investment law that includes administrative measures to protect the IP of foreign companies and ease pressure on them to transfer technology. These words did not hold much weight, however. The 12 largest Chinese companies are all state-owned and of the 109 Chinese corporations listed on the Fortune Global 500, only 15% are privately owned. Ultimately the majority of Chinese business practices are controlled by the whim of the state, for better or worse.

Decline of democracy

Too Much of a Good Thing

"The best argument against democracy is a five-minute conversation with the average voter." Winston Churchill may have seen the flaws in democracy decades ago, yet most of the upper class have been happy to bear the fruits of their flourishing democracies. Universally heralded as a pillar of stability and the champion of economic prowess, it has long been assumed that all countries would eventually turn to democracy as their wealth increased, and their political climate became more sophisticated.

Between 1988 and 2005, democracy did indeed experience a surge around the world. Since then, the tides have started to turn. The last decade has seen this trend reverse, and although democracy is still considered the foundation of prosperity around the world, its drop in popularity is currently ominously consistent. According to the Freedom of the World 2019 report, political rights and civil liberties became weaker in 68 countries since the previous year's report and improved in only 50. At the end of the 2010s, 39% of people globally, lived in countries deemed "free," while 24% lived in "partly free" countries, and 37% lived in "not free" states. Even the U.S., the "land of the free" has seen a slow but noticeable decline in its democratic score having fallen 8 points (from 94 to 86) out of a total of 100, over the past 8 years. Although this still places America firmly in the "free category," it is now falling behind its counterparts, such as the UK, Canada, France, Australia, Germany, and Japan. Figure 2 shows a graphic of the EIU's democracy ratings around the world in 2018.

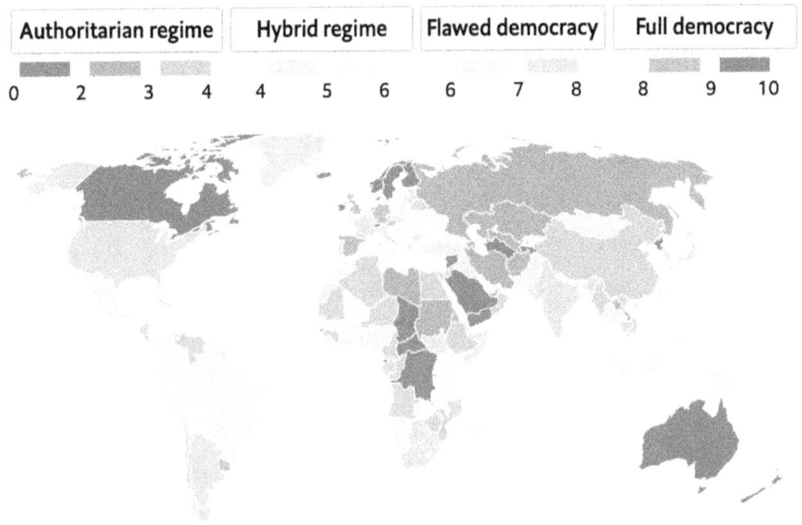

Figure 2: The EIU's Democracy Index for 167 countries around the world

The report attributes a faltering democracy in America to long-standing problems like political polarization, loss of economic mobility, the influence of special interests, and the rise of partisan media. It also warns that President Trump "exerts an influence on American politics that is straining our core values and testing the stability of our constitutional system." Still, one man alone cannot be blamed for a nation's democratic regression. Pippa Norris of the Harvard Kennedy School and the University of Sydney argues that two "twin forces" pose the largest threat to Western liberal democracies: sporadic and random terrorist attacks on domestic soil, which damage feelings of security, and the rise of populist-authoritarian forces that feed upon these fears. National anxiety then manifests into another force which tends to further threaten democracy – populism. Donald Trump's unanticipated presidential victory capitalized on this fact; he has benefited from a growing sense of mistrust of 'the establishment' and by his efforts to continually undermine faith in the legitimacy of the media and the independence of the courts. The global financial crisis notably dented the reputation of the state, and the lack of accountability for the elite financial circles that created the problem in the first stirred this resentment further.

It is, therefore, of no real surprise that populism has sprouted in the U.S. Populism can be defined as a political approach which strives to appeal to ordinary people who feel that their concerns are disregarded by established elite groups. Populism carries certain negative connotations, especially in terms of resistance to immigration, but it isn't necessarily a bad thing. In fact, history has shown that populism can play a positive role in the promotion of an electoral or minimal democracy, particularly in countries that do not currently have democratic systems in place as it can act as a stepping stone towards a more democratic state. Populism has an ironic penchant of weakening democracy, even though populism tends to favor the democratization of authoritarian regimes; it is prone to diminish the quality of established and mature liberal democracies.

A 2018 report by the Tony Blair Institute for Global Change concluded that populist rule, whether left-wing or right-wing, leads to a significant risk of democratic backsliding. The authors examined the effect of populism on three major aspects of democracy: the quality of democracy in general, checks and balances on executive power, and the citizens' right to politically participate in a meaningful way. They conclude that populist governments are four times more likely to cause harm to democratic institutions than non-populist governments. Also, more than half of populist leaders have amended or rewritten the countries' constitution in a way that frequently eroded checks and balances on executive power. Lastly, populists attack individual rights such as freedom of the press, civil liberties, and political rights. Populism can, therefore, be a way for less popular political nominees, such as Trump, to leverage the fear-induced through bad economic times and gain popularity.

The U.S. is by no means the only Western democracy to face a growing resistance. According to the Economist Intelligence Unit (EIU), democracy has declined in Europe more than in any other region in the world. Eastern Europe, in particular, has been hard hit by a growing wave of authoritarianism, and the region has deteriorated the most in 2018 since the EIU first started its Democracy Index in 2006.

The roots of Europe's democratic backsliding dig a little deeper than that of the U.S. Despite having endured the economic hardships of the global financial crises and sovereign debt crises, mass immigration across much of the continent stirred resentment further. Drought, poverty, and war have accelerated large-scale migration to Europe from the Middle East and Africa (MENA). According to the United Nations High Commissioner for Refugees, the top three nationalities of entrants of the over one million Mediterranean Sea arrivals between January 2015 and March 2016 were Syrian (46.7%), Afghan (20.9%) and Iraqi (9.4%), three countries hit particularly hard by civil wars. Mass immigration, combined with deteriorating economic opportunities, has left a bad taste in many a Europeans' mouth. Immigrants unfairly bear the brunt of much of this hatred. Once again, populist leaders and parties have used (and often abused) circumstantial events involving immigrants for their own personal political agendas. Germany has fallen foul to this type of behavior, as evidenced in the 2015-2016 New Year's Eve sexual assaults. Despite these criminals representing only a small proportion of all immigrants, the media has portrayed all other immigrants as guilty by association.

On 4 January 2016, the police president of Cologne announced that during the last New Year's Eve's celebrations, a great number of young men "of appearance largely from the north African or Arab world" had in groups sexually assaulted "a very large number" of women in Cologne's city center. The next day, the police of Hamburg issued a similar statement and outlined the incidents in Stuttgart to international news media. On 6 January, German news media reported sexual assaults on New Year's Eve by "immigrants" in Bielefeld and Dortmund by large groups of men with a poor command of the German or English language. By January 7th, international media reported "similar incidents" in Frankfurt and Düsseldorf. As tragic as these events were, the true scale of the attacks was greatly inflated. These isolated incidents allowed the media to add fuel to the fire, worsening public perception of refugees for fear of losing their country and national identity.

Despite a rise in popularity for Germany's right-wing populist, Alternative for Germany (AfD) party, its strong democratic backbone has managed to prevail. Yet other countries have not been so successful. Hungary is an example of a country where a large group of unemployed, low-educated people were dissatisfied with high levels of inequality, especially after the financial crisis of 2007–2008. Viktor Orbán, Hungary's newly elected Prime Minister, capitalized on the dissatisfaction of one of the larger segments of the Hungarian population, winning popular support by employing national-populist rhetoric.

As is common with many populist leaders, Viktor Orbán has since presided over one of the most dramatic declines in democracy ever recorded, as charted by Freedom House within the European Union. Having worked methodically to deny critical voices a platform in the media or civil society, Orbán and his right-wing nationalist Fidesz party easily defended their parliamentary supermajority in the 2018 elections. Soon after, the government forced the closure of the Central European University and evicted its vibrant academic community. Unsurprisingly, the year ended with vigorous dissent from thousands of protesters who took to the streets to denounce Orbán's abuses, where they were met with state violence and police brutality. Unfortunately, Hungary is not an isolated example of European democratic regression. Populist parties in Europe have tripled their vote in the past 20 years. Eleven European countries are now represented by populist parties, and more than a quarter of Europeans voted for a populist in their last elections.

Italian politics took a sharp turn when a populist government coalition between the anti-establishment Five Star Movement and right-wing League party ceded control, proceeding to swiftly drop its democracy ranking from 21st in 2017 to 33rd just a year later. A global wave of autocratization (a reduction in democratic qualities that can lead to the breakdown of democracy) occurred over much of Eastern Europe, notably in Turkey, Poland, Ukraine, and Russia. Russia, perhaps as predicted, was ranked the least democratic country in Europe, obtaining 144th place on the global chart below countries such as Afghanistan and Zimbabwe.

Nonetheless, it is not all doom and gloom for Europe. Despite the widely reported "democratic malaise," many European countries still dominate the list of most democratic countries in the world with Norway ranking first, followed closely by Iceland and Sweden. Despite dealing with rising levels of immigration, Finland, Germany, and Malta also increased their scores towards the end of 2018. Figure 3 provides a list for the top 10 most democratic countries in the world as of 2018, of which 70% are European.

Rank	Country
1	Norway
2	Iceland
3	Sweden
4	New Zealand
5	Denmark
6	Canada
7	Ireland
8	Finland
9	Australia
10	Switzerland

Figure 3. Top 10 most democratic countries in the world as of 2018

On another note, the manner in which Brexit is being executed by the UK's new eccentric Prime Minister, Boris Johnson, will prove extremely divisive and could lead to increasing political polarization and, ultimately, a loss of confidence in democracy in the UK. Close attention must also be paid to the rising populist parties in Sweden and Spain.

The next decade will be a critical one for the future of democracy. In recent years, global threats to democracy have emerged with prominence. The signs seem clear: The Arab spring fizzled. China's leader is poised to rule for life. America and Britain, long seen as prime examples of successful democracies throughout the world, have become pinched by internal warring factions. Developing countries from the Middle East and Africa are noticing how democracies can lose their vigor whilst authoritarian states such as China and Russia are able to retain control and flourish economically. In the democracy's battle for survival, it is important to remember what exactly is being fought for. As Franklin D. Roosevelt once quipped: "Let us never forget that government is ourselves and not an alien power over us. The ultimate rulers of our democracy are not a President and senators and congressmen and government officials, but the voters of this country".

Arab Spring

A Leopard Cannot Change its Spots

Eighteen countries, 180,000 deaths, and 6 million displaced civilians. These are just a few of the shocking statistics of what is perhaps one of the most alarming yet severely underreported political events of the past decade. Coined the "Arab Spring," the series of anti-government protests, uprisings, and rebellions that spanned the entirety of North Africa and much of the Middle East in the early 2010s have mostly died out. Yet, the resulting political, social, and economic damages can still be felt throughout the region today. Despite the lack of media coverage by the Western world, the Arab Spring is often thought to be the biggest transformation of the Middle East since decolonization.

The spark that ignited this fire can be traced back to Tunisia in December 2010, following the death of the Tunisian street vendor Mohamed Bouazizi. A college-educated street vendor, Mohamed lit himself on fire. He burned to death due to despair and frustration from joblessness and little hope of prosperity, which is a common plight for many young and educated people in Tunisia. Mohamed's ultimate sacrifice proved to be the catalyst in mobilizing people to protest for change. Whilst this initial wave of protests in Tunisia was in response to a low standard of living and little economic hope, it soon turned into something much bigger, with millions of people revolting against an oppressive regime and a corrupt political landscape emboldened by cronyism, fraud, and bureaucracy. The death of the "Tunisian Burning Man" initiated an intensive 28-day campaign of civil resistance called the Tunisian Revolution. The series of street protests aimed to remove the long-time president Zine

El Abidine Ben Ali from his 23 years of abusive power where he amassed quite the rap sheet, having now been charged with money laundering, drug trafficking and, in 2012, he was sentenced to life imprisonment in absentia, for inciting violence, murder and for the violent repression of protests. Ben Ali fled to Jeddah, Saudi Arabia, where he is now being harbored under King Abdullah.

Within just one month of the self-immolation of Mohamed Bouazizi, Tunisian president Ben Ali was replaced, and a new democracy ushered in. Despite Tunisia having endured horrific terror attacks and economic woes, the removal of the corrupt autocrat, together with the introduction of a genuine democracy, served as a beacon of hope to other oppressed groups throughout the region.

The seeming success of the Tunisian Revolution soon spread fiercely to five other countries: Libya, Egypt, Yemen, Syria, and Bahrain. The successive waves of protests around the region all centered around a few key agendas. Essentially, the series of Arab Spring uprisings revolved around young generations attempting to peacefully protest against corrupt, oppressive, and socially destructive authoritarian regimes, with the ultimate aim to secure a more democratic political system and hence, a brighter economic future. Other important factors included incompetent monarchies, human rights violations, economic decline, and overly high levels of unemployment and poverty. Weary and poor groups of educated but unemployed protestors, who were rendered idle due to a weak economy and inherent lack of opportunity, proved one of the key motivating factors in mobilizing these crowds.

The initial wave of protests in other countries spurred on by Tunisia's apparent quick success appeared promising. In Egypt, President Hosni Mubarak resigned in February 2011 after 18 days of wide-scale and unrelenting protests, which ended his crippling 30-year rule. The Libyan leader Muammar Gadaffi was famously overthrown in August 2011, followed by his brutal death shortly after by the National Traditional Council (NTC), who tracked him down in his hometown, savagely beat him to death and paraded his corpse around town to roars of applause by locals. By the end of 2012, just a couple of years after the spark of protests in Tunisia, incompetent rulers had been forced from power in Tunisia, Egypt, Libya, and Yemen, with further civil uprisings erupting in Bahrain and Syria. Major protests also broke out in Algeria, Iraq, Jordan, Kuwait, Morocco, Oman, and Sudan along with minor protests in neighboring regions.

Although coups and political tugs-of-war have been occurring in the Middle East and Africa for thousands of years, the scale of the Arab Spring uprisings erupting in 2010 was mostly caused by a new modern externality that has become an increasingly important yet controversial factor, especially in the last decade - social media.

Social media has proved to be a vital tool in the mass mobilization of protestors over the last decade. News outlets have heralded social media as the driving force for change, enabling successful large-scale protests by ordinary citizens against their oppressive ruling elites. As victories emerge, such as the ousting of the Egyptian and Tunisian Presidents in the early 2010s, news spreads quickly to other regions, offering tangible proof that mass protests and activist movements can evoke real change. The use of social media platforms more than doubled in Arab states during the protests. Dominant platforms, such as Facebook and Twitter, played a key role in organizing protests within Tunisia and Egypt, which ultimately led to the ousting of their oppressive leaders. Polls suggest that 9 out of 10 Egyptians and Tunisians used Facebook to spread awareness and organize protests.

As much as the power of social media can be harnessed to organize protests and create a voice for the people, it can be equally powerful to those trying to suppress them. In many countries, particularly those involved in the Arab Spring, governments have identified the role of social media for protest-organizing. They have been known to shut down certain sites (Facebook, Twitter, etc.) or block access to the internet altogether, much to the detriment of its citizens. In addition to blocking and preventing communication between protestors, ruling parties are also known for using social media to push their own agendas, usually through accusing others and peddling propaganda that is completely and undeniably fabricated. Figure 4 shows a graphic of countries with some of the least press freedom, of which North Africa and the Middle East rank particularly low.

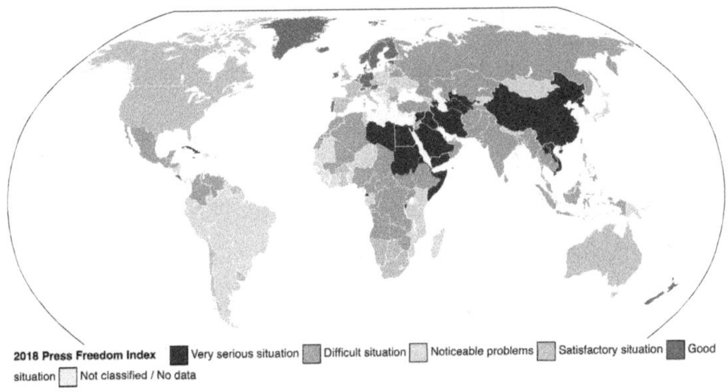

Figure 4: 2018 Press Freedom Index.

The initial wave of revolutions and protests had mostly faded by mid-2012, as Tunisia's and Egypt's success in overthrowing their oppressive regimes rang fresh in the minds of other political parties who feared similar activist movements. In a bid to prevent the reoccurrence of such mutiny, many protest movements across the Arab Springs were met with extreme violence and state brutality. These attacks were sometimes met with retaliating protestor violence, leading to many arrests, injuries, and deaths of mostly innocent citizens. As the initial waves of revolution and regime change rapidly unfolded, it brought with it dangerous power struggles. Whilst leadership changed, and ruling elites were held accountable, the lack of competent successors resulted in power vacuums across the Arab world. Consequently, constant warring between factions vying for whatever power they could grasp ensued, particularly by groups of elites trying to establish new hybrid regimes based on religion and a new demand for democracy.

Some of the most brutal and heartbreaking events of the Arab Spring were witnessed in Syria, where the protests which started in January 2011 have only recently started to subside, in spite of the failure to oust the brutal regime of the infamous authoritarian Bashar al-Assad. A chain reaction of events, starting with the assault of a Damascus citizen by a police officer, and the subsequent arrest of those who peacefully protested for his release, resulted in an eruption of protests against the state, which had been ruling Syria since 1963. Many protests were held in the subsequent months, most met with state brutality almost unimaginable in the Western world. Among the incidents was the fateful day when Syrian security forces opened fire on ambulances carrying injured citizens away, killing 11 people, including the paramedics.

In response to such state brutality, bands of rebels fueled by a passionate distaste of state brutality responded with violence of their own. The Free Syrian Army was one of the most determined of such groups. Resistance against state forces resulted in a civil war that soon spread further afield, dragging in bigger nations such as Russia and Turkey, who had agendas of their own. The U.S. tried (albeit meekly) to instill some form of order in the area via drone strikes and targeted bombing campaigns, but ultimately failed to yield any tangible results and made life much harder for Syrian citizens trying to cling to whatever sense of normality they could find. Eight years later, the country is a complete shell, with many major cities completely desolate and occupied only by rubble. With the backing of Russia, who has its own agenda in the Middle East, Bashar al-Assad has stripped his country bare and has committed heinous war crimes, including multiple uses of chemical weapons and state-sanctioned torture on Syrian citizens. Although the worst seems to be finally over, the situation is compounded by Trump's decision to withdraw 1,000 U.S. Special Forces troops from the region. The critical risk here is that the terrorist organization ISIS, the reason U.S. troops were deployed into Syria in the first place, may use this vacuum of security to regain ground.

Looking back over the past decade of activity in the Arab Spring, the result is bittersweet. The intentions were certainly noble and worthy of pursuit, with the aim of a fair democracy, better economic conditions and living standards a benefit for everyone. Early protests in Tunisia and Egypt can certainly be looked upon with a certain degree of success, where corrupt and incompetent presidents have been ousted, and modern political parties are increasingly in tune with the new demands of its people. Yet, earlier hopes that these popular movements, which would bring about greater economic equality, end corruption and increase political participation, have not come to fruition after nearly a decade.

Despite all the political activity and change of governments across dozens of countries, only Tunisia – the cradle of the Arab Spring – can claim a successful transition to democracy. It has been a long and arduous transition. To date, Tunisia is still dealing with religious extremism and a weak economy, which put the rise of a strong middle class and a stable democracy at a standstill. Still, the fact that Tunisia has survived such a difficult transition offers a beacon of light in such murky times.

One could liken the ousting of President Hosni Mubarak in Egypt to the earlier success of Tunisia. Replacing the incompetent incumbent was Islamist Mohamed Morsi, who was himself later deposed in a coup in 2013 and replaced by the current president General Abdel Fattah El-Sisi during protests that killed over 800 people. Whilst initially popular, General El-Sisi proves himself to be a ruthless and repressive leader, who bans any form of public criticism of the country or its rulers and routinely encourages state torture of detainees with little to no accountability for violations of the law.

Oppressive regimes like that of Egypt are an all too familiar scene for many Middle-eastern countries. In Libya, where former Prime Minister Muammar Gadaffi was dragged to a sewer drain and butchered to death in 2011, an ensuing power void resulted in intense factional wars between different groups of rebels, all seeking to gain and fill in the vacancy of authority. Libya is still yet to recover from this historical moment and has been suffering ever since. The current state is still crippled and houses the worst violations of human freedom and equality. Criminality and human trafficking are so rampant that gangs hold public slave auctions, and every year, thousands of desperate migrants from sub-Saharan Africa are forced onto decrepit boats for the risky trip to Europe where many have been swallowed up by the Mediterranean Sea. The European Union has been accused of fueling conflict by paying Libyan militias to crack down on trafficking routes. The number of people crossing the sea has hence dropped, but thousands are still trapped in the state and are suffering in makeshift prisons built for nothing but misery.

Whilst internal conflicts across the dozens of affected countries have subsided, the transition to democracy is still far from complete. One external factor, which often goes unnoticed, has ultimately made it almost impossible for such progress to be made. Meddling by foreign state actors, especially religious zealots whose sole goal is Islamist "state-building," actively seek areas where power voids have been created. The most prominent of these states have been in Iraq, Syria, Yemen, and Libya. To back their own agendas, external players such as the United Arab Emirates (UAE) and Saudi Arabia have rallied around a pan-Islamic identity, supplying weapons and fighters to secure these areas under Islamic control. The norms of governance in these Islamist areas are militia-based, with the governed submitting to the authorities out of fear or blind loyalty. The most notable of these new governance models is the Islamic State (IS), whose brutal interpretation of Islam has resulted in some of the cruelest events incomparable to the medieval period. This has also led to an increase in sectarianism and infighting amongst Islamists themselves, especially Sunni-Shia conflicts which have fueled the catastrophic civil wars in Lebanon, Yemen, and Iraq. The increasing influence from Middle Eastern authoritative figures also risks dragging in Western counterparts, not unlike Syria's case, which may further prolong the infighting, pain, and suffering.

Today, the region seems even further than its initial noble call for democratized and ideal-utopian societies, which bellowed across the Middle East and Africa, presenting a glimmer of hope in, particularly, depressing times. With only one lasting democratic shift in Tunisia, it is difficult to justify the merciless massacres, waves of mass emigration, and total annihilation of many historic and once prosperous cities. Perhaps it is the price to pay in the long transition to a better, more democratic future. Although the Arab Spring, as we know it may be over, the underlying political and social activism most certainly isn't. Current authoritarian nations have learned to control political activism and resist protests through increased brutality, repression of dissent, state terrorism, and help from external suppressive states. This does not sound like a model of stability, however. Soon the tides will change, the cracks will form, and the Arab Spring, or whatever future form it takes, will evolve likely into something bigger and uglier than before.

Nuclear Proliferation

One Step Forward and Two Steps Back...

To say there are too many nuclear weapons in the world is an understatement. The world's largest nuclear weapon ever created was the Russian engineered "Tsar bomb," rated at a cataclysmic 50 megatons of pure destruction. To put this into perspective, this single eight-meter and twenty-seven-ton mass of pure carnage contains the collective number of explosives used during World War II, multiplied by ten. The now 60-year-old weapon was tested in 1961 with a mushroom cloud reaching over 40 miles high, turning miles upon miles of Arctic ground into literal dust. With an explosive area of 950 square miles, just 4,200 Tsar bombs would be needed to scorch the entire surface of the US, and perhaps as few as 100-200 strategically targeted bombs to completely cripple it. There are an estimated 15,000 nuclear weapons in the world today.

Fortunately, this number is much less than the 70,000 bombs stockpiled after escalating global tensions from the Cold War in 1986. Further progress towards continued denuclearization has since been made, with the idea of a totally nuclear-free world seemingly in agreement across the globe.

The past decade has seen substantial progress between the two superpowers most likely to be involved in some form of nuclear war. On 8 April 2010, the United States and Russia signed a treaty to reduce both parties' stockpiles of atomic weapons by half, after years of arduous negotiations between Barack Obama and Dmitry

Medvedev. This new treaty replaced the outdated but effective Strategic Offensive Reductions Treaty (SORT), which was set to expire. The treaty went into force in February 2011 after it was ratified by both nations and was promisingly named "New START (Strategic Arms Reduction Treaty). It is expected to last until 2021, where upon mutual agreement, a 5-yearly extension can be added. The treaty aims to gradually remove the threat of nuclear escalation by removing nuclear weapons from both sides. This treaty ensures that neither party is at more of a disadvantage than the other and that both experience increased benefit from harboring fewer weapons in total. The concept is similar to the removal of guns from a mid-western dual; since neither has a weapon to attack with, both are less likely to be killed.

Under the terms of the new treaty, the number of strategic nuclear missile launchers should be reduced by half through the establishment of a new inspection and verification regime. It does not, however, limit the number of operationally inactive stockpiled nuclear warheads that number in the high thousands in both Russian and American inventories. The numerical limit on the number of deployed strategic nuclear warheads was set to 1,550, down nearly two-thirds from the previous START treaty. It also limits the number of deployed and undeployed inter-continental ballistic missile (ICBM) launchers, submarine-launched ballistic missile (SLBM) launchers, and heavy bombers equipped for nuclear armaments to a total of 800. To ensure these limits are abided by, the treaty calls for ongoing satellite and remote monitoring as well as 18 on-site inspections per year.

Documents made available to the U.S. Senate described the removal of at least 30 missile silos, 34 bombers, and 56 submarine launch tubes from service. Seven years after the New START treaty was enforced, the two countries have declared that they have met the prescribed limits. This news, at a time when relations between the two countries are at a post-Cold War low, and defense hawks in both countries are screaming for new nuclear weapons and declaring arms control dead, couldn't be more timely or important. The deal has been heralded a mighty achievement and great success. Figure 5 shows the reduction in certain types of heavy weapons between 2011 and 2018.

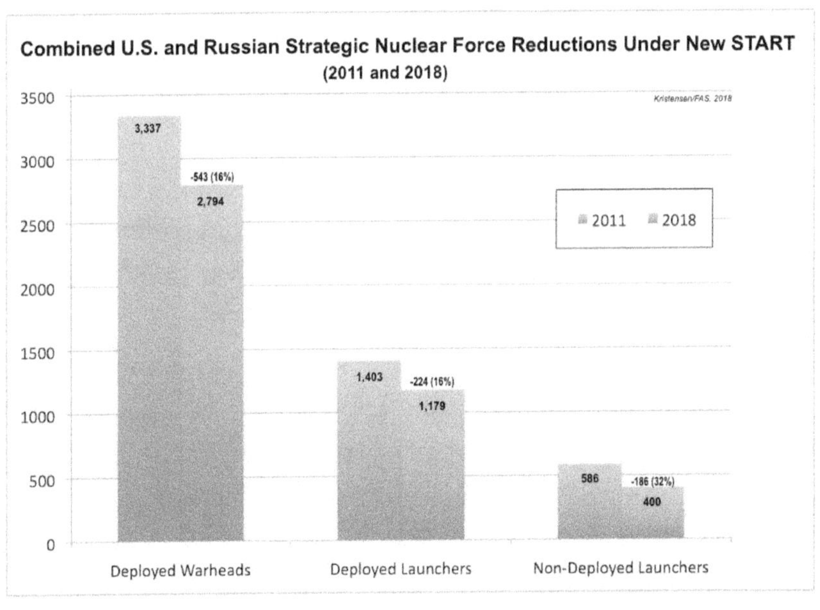

Figure 5: Reduction in deployed and non-deployed weapons from 2011 to 2018.

Then came Donald Trump. According to a Reuters report on February 9, 2017, during U.S. President Donald Trump's first 60-minute telephone call with Russian President Vladimir Putin, Putin inquired about extending New START. President Trump attacked the treaty, claiming that it favored Russia and was "one of several bad deals negotiated by the Obama administration." Another previous success story between the two disarming nations, the Intermediate-Range Nuclear Forces (INF) Treaty, was also nullified by Donald Trump, thus raising concerns on the future of nuclear arms control. The U.S. formally suspended the nuclear treaty on 1 February 2019, causing Russia to do the same and very quickly undoing a decade's work of making the world a safer place for all.

The election of Donald Trump in 2016 reintroduced a nuclear threat back into the Middle East. America and much of the western world, for that matter, had been trying to quash a nuclear threat present since the 1980s, and it seemed as though the threat had finally been contained. In 2015, Iran and other world powers agreed to trade sanctions relief for explicit constraints on Iran's contentious nuclear program, including allowing inspections of nuclear facilities by the International Atomic Energy Agency (IAEA). Iran, desperate to exploit its vast and lucrative oil exports, willingly complied, and great progress was made in dismantling Iran's nuclear facilities. In early 2016 the IAEA confirmed that Iran had complied with the agreement, allowing the United Nations to lift sanctions immediately. However, on May 8, 2018, President Donald Trump announced the United States was withdrawing from the deal.

The origin of the Iranian nuclear threat started in 1979 after Iranian students stormed the U.S. Embassy in Tehran and held American diplomats hostage. Immediately after, the U.S. imposed sanctions on Iran, banning imports to the U.S. and effectively freezing $12 billion in Iranian assets. After 5 years of a deteriorating relationship, the U.S. declared Iran a state sponsor of terrorism for repeatedly providing "support for acts of international terrorism", and imposed further U.S. sanctions. For a "state sponsor of terrorism" to enrich uranium (which can be used to arm nuclear weapons) was of grave concern, so under the office of Barack Obama, a group called the P5+1 was formed. This group comprised of the United States, the United Kingdom, Russia, France, China, the European Union (EU) and Germany. In 2015, the sanctions relief was agreed upon by all, and Iran was shown to have reduced its enrichment of uranium.

Despite tearing up the agreement, Trump's exit from the pact has not completely voided the deal. All remaining constituents of the P5+1 have agreed to uphold the deal without U.S. input. It is unclear what Iran plans to do next however. Iranian President Hassan Rouhani said in response to Trump's announcement that Tehran would remain in the nuclear agreement without Washington for now but reserved the right to resume enriching uranium if negotiations fell apart. The U.S.'s violation of the agreement is at risk of being seized by Iranian hardliners as evidence that the U.S. cannot be trusted, thereby leaving Iran with no choice but to abandon the deal and resume its nuclear enrichment program. Leaders like Rouhani and others associated with the deal "are under a lot of pressure and are facing a great deal of criticism for being naive for trusting the United States." This does not bode well for an already shaky EU, which can hardly hope to keep the nuclear agreement afloat if it can't persuade Iran to continue its commitment to the deal. The Iran nuclear deal provided a small glimmer of good news in a region bounded by war and suffering for most of the past decade. Only time will tell if this much needed ray of hope can be salvaged.

Despite revoking one nuclear deal, Trump can perhaps be credited with assuaging another. North Korea and the "little rocket man" Kim Jong Un have engaged in a serious game of "nuclear Russian roulette." In addition to stockpiling significant quantities of chemical and biological weapons, as of 2019, North Korea is estimated to have an arsenal of approximately 20 to 30 nuclear weapons and sufficient fissile material for an additional 30 to 60.

North Korea's relations with much of the world started to significantly deteriorate in 2003 when North Korea withdrew from the Treaty on the Non-Proliferation of Nuclear Weapons (NPT). Since 2006, the country has been conducting a series of nuclear tests at increasing levels of expertise, prompting other countries, particularly the U.S. and China, to demand sanctions.

The last decade has seen this nuclear threat from the North Korean regime escalate, especially after a series of earthquakes with a magnitude of around 5 were detected in the region, signifying nuclear weapons testing. Additionally, in July 2017, North Korea launched Hwasong-14 from a mobile intercontinental ballistic missile, with a claimed lofted trajectory of 39 minutes, which landed in the waters of the Japanese exclusive economic zone. U.S. Pacific Command confirmed the missile was aloft for 37 minutes, which suggested that in a standard trajectory, it could have reached across all of Alaska – meaning a distance of 4,160 miles. Just a month later, North Korea launched a second ICBM that was apparently more advanced with an altitude of around 2300 miles. Analysts estimated that it was capable of reaching the continental United States.

Following claims that North Korea had successfully tested a thermonuclear bomb, otherwise known as a hydrogen bomb (and evidenced by a magnitude 6.3 earthquake), U.S. President Donald Trump announced that North Korea was re-listed by the State Department as a state sponsor of terrorism. Japan and South Korea welcomed the move as a method of increasing pressure on North Korea to partake in denuclearization negotiations. In response, North Korea has repeatedly threatened the United States, South Korea, and Japan with pre-emptive nuclear strikes.

It was, therefore, a surprising yet welcomed turn of events when North Korea suddenly announced in 2018 that they may disarm their nuclear arsenal after negotiations with the United States. Pragmatically, Trump accepted the offer of talks, ignoring past pre-talk conditions that North Korea denuclearize first. After a series of much-publicized talks, the two signed an agreement committing to the "complete denuclearization of the Korean peninsula" but with no detail on what that would contain. In essence, the U.S. suggested that North Korea unilaterally give up its nuclear weapons while Pyongyang desired a step-by-step approach to ease the crippling sanctions regime. As many had predicted, the talks have not amassed to much concrete change. After the two leaders met for a second summit in Hanoi, talks once again broke down, after which North Korea carried out new weapons tests, which were seen as an attempt to increase pressure on the U.S.

Whatever the intention, Trump's newfound enthusiasm for diplomacy has temporarily lowered the temperature on the Korean Peninsula. Still, it also highlights a bigger question: does the U.S. have a strategy for North Korea, or are these twists and turns merely the whims of a capricious president? North Korea has all but completed its quest for nuclear weapons and the result is a heightened danger in the U.S.–North Korean relationship, a high-stakes nuclear standoff. Regardless of whether diplomacy ensues or the United States turns its focus to other tools—sanctions, deterrence, or even military force—the same underlying challenge will remain: the outcome of this standoff will be determined by how each country can influence the other.

Notable Figures

Donald Trump

Hot Shot or Hot Air?

Love or hate him; one thing about Donald Trump cannot be denied – he is certainly a force to be reckoned with. Trump is simultaneously an unstoppable force and an immovable object that has made a parody of the seemingly boring field of politics, arousing daily discussions worldwide. Whilst he is almost certainly one of the most polarizing presidents in American history, this brief summary will outline his impact as objectively as possible. In a world of "fake news" and seemingly brainwashed supporters, it is rare that an unbiased and fact-based analysis of his life and presidency is presented.

As the 45th president of the U.S., Trump has already set many firsts. Firstly, he is the oldest elected president at the age of 70. He is also the first elected president who did not serve in the military or hold elective or appointed government office before his election. This in no way determines a good or bad president, however. In fact, a change from bureaucrats is welcome and was one of his campaign's key strengths. Lastly, and perhaps unsurprisingly, he is the wealthiest president ever to be elected.

Since first gaining public prominence, Trump has always been known for his extreme wealth. The Trump Organization LLC acts as the central holding company for his vast array of companies and is his primary source of wealth, focusing mainly on large scale real estate developments such as skyscrapers, hotels, golf courses, and casinos. Contrary to popular belief, Trump does not own many of the buildings which bear his name, rather he leases his name out through licensing agreements. Trump is estimated to own around 500 companies in the U.S. alone, including some unusual businesses with products ranging from perfume to spring water and steaks. In 2019, Forbes estimated Trump's net worth at around $3.1 billion, making him one of the richest politicians in American history and the first American billionaire president. His successful career in business was one of his main selling points for his presidential campaign, where he planned to apply the same shrewd business formula to becoming an equally successful president.

Alas, it is fair to say it has been harder for Trump than he might have expected. Despite his stunning win from a position of total weakness in the largest presidential primary field for any political party in American History, his early success has been hindered by wave after wave of allegations, including sexual harassment allegations and suspected collusion with Russia and Ukraine. These claims are at the heart of his ongoing impeachment inquiries. His political stance is that of a populist, protectionist, and nationalist, a perfectly timed position appealing to many demographics who fear mass immigration and who cling to a strong sense of national heritage. Despite losing the popular vote (he received fewer overall votes than Hilary Clinton), his campaign team better executed their plan to win specific key states that ultimately proved vital. On the flip side, his polarizing figure and brash demeanor have made him a magnet for lots of negative attention, a lot of which is his own undoing. However, like any president, he has his good policies.

The Good...

The annexation of Crimea (a pro-Russian Ukrainian peninsula) by Russia was a terrible breach of peace by a bully nation who got away with it simply because no-one else had an interest in stepping up to fight them. Never one to back down from a fight, Trump's party has stepped up to address this brazen injustice, in direct opposition to allegations of Russian collusion during the 2016 election. The Secretary of Defense, James Mattis, acknowledges that U.S. instructors are training Ukrainian military units at a base in western Ukraine. Washington had also approved two important arms sales to Kiev's ground forces in the past nine months. The first transaction in December 2017 was limited to small arms that at least could be portrayed as purely for defensive purposes, including the export of Model M107A1 Sniper Systems, ammunition, and associated parts and accessories. The sale was valued at $41.5 million.

A second transaction in April 2018 was more dire. Not only was it a larger transaction ($47 million), it included far more lethal weaponry, such as the 210 Javelin anti-tank missiles, which Barack Obama's administration had previously declined to give Kiev. Needless to say, the Kremlin was not pleased about both sales. Following that, the U.S. Congress passed legislation in May that authorized around $250 million in military assistance including lethal weaponry for Ukraine in 2019. Congress had twice voted for military support on a similar scale during the last years of Obama's administration, but the White House blocked implementation. The Trump administration cleared that obstacle in December 2017 at the same time that it approved the initial small-weapons sale. The passage of the May 2018 legislation means that the path is now open for an expansion of U.S. military backing for Kiev. By standing up for smaller and bullied nations, the current U.S. administration hopes to make others wary of making such drastic and aggressive moves, hopefully reducing the likelihood and severity of bullying in the future.

Trump's helping hand extends to other countries too, such as in crisis-ridden Venezuela, where he recognized Juan Guaido as the legitimate president of Venezuela in a bid to remove the corrupt dictator Nicholas Maduro. Maduro had been accused of several despicable crimes against humanity, and his ousting could not have happened without American backing, allowing Guaido to replace the tyrant, although the fight for the Venezuelan presidency is still ongoing. Other under-the-radar policies implemented by Trump include the child and daycare tax credit in the U.S., which enables parents to receive tax credits for a percentage of the cost spent on daycare and childcare, making it easier for mothers to return to the workforce and encouraging a larger portion of women to seek employment.

Trump's purported brash and reckless persona, bizarrely allowed him to curry favor with one of the most delicate and fragile relationships in Asia, North Korea. Despite decades of his predecessors trying to appease the small and combative state, Trump and Kim Jong Un seemed to have hit it off. For years, North Korea worried most of the world with their accumulation and testing of nuclear weapons. Many prior administrations failed to make any contact, let alone progress, with the authoritarian region. Despite his abrasive character, Trump became the first sitting president to ever meet a North Korean leader.

Despite initial talks appearing to make progress, talks broke down in February 2019, although both sides say they still intend to continue the discussion. Regardless, the fact that the verbal barrier has now been broken is more progress than any other president has managed to achieve to date.

Perhaps Trump's biggest legacy, however, is the ongoing trade wars with many key economies, including former allies. Many tariffs are aimed at countries where both parties would benefit from more trade and not less, such as Canada, Mexico, and Europe. Still, the escalating tariffs with China appear damaging but are arguably necessary, which is a point Trump's administration has emphasized throughout his tenure.

Trump also initiated a series of trade actions in January 2018, beginning with tariffs on imported washing machines and solar panels, followed later in March by tariffs on imported steel and aluminum from most countries, which later included economic allies like Canada, Mexico, and the European Union. In July, Trump ramped up his assault on China by imposing tariffs on 818 categories of Chinese goods worth $50 billion, triggering a series of escalating tariffs between the two countries over the ensuing months that soon became characterized as a trade war. Several countries, including China, Mexico, Canada, the European Union, India, and Turkey, imposed retaliatory tariffs on American exports – in some cases, they were specifically targeted at Trump's political base. After negotiations between China and the United States failed to resolve the trade conflict, Trump executed his earlier threat to impose tariffs on another $200 billion of Chinese goods.

Whilst placing trade restrictions on allies was at best questionable, Trump's tariffs on China was a long time coming. Poor business ethics by the corrupt Chinese state, along with a lack of democratic freedoms and laws, have allowed China's key businesses and industries to act according to their personal political agendas. This is now estimated to have cost the U.S. hundreds of millions of dollars in lost intellectual property. Xi Jinping's reaction was to increase the transparency of the Chinese business landscape and open up the economy to foreign investment, hopefully reducing the handing over of IP and safeguarding U.S. business practices. Although a trade war may not be the most efficient method in improving business relations, Trump's display of non-conformity to China's whims supports his stance that the U.S. must not bow to the pressures of a foreign power and hold its own impending despite consequences, as Trump has.

The Bad...

It seems fair to say that Trump's presidency did not get off to the best of starts. The first major policy of his tenure was the implementation of a travel ban on citizens from several Muslim-majority countries for which he cited national security concerns. While later amending his banning criteria from Muslim countries to mainly terrorist bases, the racist undertones left a nasty impression on most of the American public and the Supreme Court, which turned down the policy twice. After major revisions, the ban has now been upheld by the Supreme court in its third revision, where foreigners from six majority-Muslim countries must now have a "bona fide" relationship to a person or entity to enter the U.S. Whilst genuine security concerns are an important topic to all Americans, the way it was implemented through Islamophobic rhetoric ultimately proved damaging to Trump's already suffering credibility.

Despite his trade war with China, deemed a necessary action among the general consensus, the extension of this "America First" protectionism to other countries has created tensions where none were necessary. In March 2018, Trump's administration-imposed tariffs of 25% on steel and 10% on aluminum, extending to previous trade allies such as Canada, Mexico, and the EU. In response, tariffs were imposed on the U.S., creating a standoff where everyone involved made losses.

Despite the tariffs' goal of reducing the U.S. trade deficit, the consensus among analysts – including Trump's top economic advisor, Larry Kudlow – is that the Trump tariffs have had a small to moderately negative effect on GDP growth. Between President Trump's 2017 inauguration and 2019, the U.S.'s trade deficit had grown by $119 billion. In March 2019, the U.S. Department of Commerce stated that in 2018, the trade deficit reached $621 billion, at its highest since 2008. Numerous papers from The Economist, the Peterson Institute for International Economics, and Deutsche Bank have all come to similar conclusions. American businesses and consumers are estimated to have paid $900,000 a year for each job that was created or saved as a result of the Trump administration's tariffs on steel and aluminum.

Analysis conducted by CNBC in May 2019 found that Trump

"enacted tariffs equivalent to one of the largest tax increases in decades," while the Tax Foundation and Tax Policy Center analyses found the tariffs could offset the benefits of the Tax Cuts and Jobs Act of 2017 for many households. The Tax Foundation found that if all existing and proposed tariffs were fully implemented, the benefits of the Trump tax cut would be completely eliminated for all taxpayers through the 90th percentile in earnings. Calling the Trump tariffs "an extraordinary abuse of taxing authority," a May 2019 analysis conducted by the National Taxpayers Union found that the existing and proposed additional tariffs if fully implemented, would constitute the largest tax increase of the post-war era. It seems despite his "America First" protectionist intentions, it is the American taxpayer that is bearing the brunt.

Other policies generally viewed as negative include pulling out of the Iran nuclear deal, which enables the country to now enrich as much nuclear material as it wants, without repercussions from previous U.S. sanctions that kept Iran's nuclear weapons experimentation in check.

Team Trump has also pulled out of the Paris Accord agreement, which is a collective effort among able countries aiming to strengthen the global response to the threat of climate change. The agreement includes the responsibility of keeping a global temperature rise within this century well below 2 degrees Celsius above pre-industrial levels. While Trump may be right in that the agreement is flawed, his lack of a proposed alternative and general absence of care for what is widely believed to become the greatest existential threat to mankind is deeply worrying.

The Ugly...

Whilst politicians and their policies can be argued to their merit or discredit by various groups, perhaps the biggest contributing factor to Trump's low popularity is his demeanor and apparent lack of any moral fiber.

Even before he was elected, footage emerged of his arrogant and chauvinistic view towards women with recorded comments such as "I just start kissing them ... I don't even wait. And when you're a star, they let you do it, you can do anything ... grab 'em by the pussy.", which he passed off as simply "locker room talk." It got much worse from there, however. To date, twenty-two women have publicly accused Trump of sexual misconduct.

Trump was alleged to have been violent to his victims, kissing and groping some without their consent and was even accused of rape. Two days before the second presidential debate in October 2016, a recording surfaced of Trump openly bragging about forcibly kissing and groping women. Many similar allegations have also been made about many of Trump's closest aides and personal friends, including Jeffrey Epstein, who was accused in 2019 of running a child prostitution ring before his mysterious 'suicide' in a Manhattan jail cell.

Trump facilitated the widespread use of a new phrase: fake news. Although the American media does have a history of misinformation and "not letting the truth get in the way of a good story," Trump has simply brushed off all negative information on himself as "fake news." This churlish and see-through act, however, has become very effective for Trump, who has fended off some of the most serious criminal and fraudulent accusations that would see most other people locked up in a prison cell. What awaits him when he steps down as president, however, must cause him quite a few sleepless nights.

Vladimir Putin

From Russia with Love

Despite a successful decade in the noughties, the 2010s has not been kind to Russian President Vladimir Putin. His first and second presidential terms between 2000 and 2008 couldn't have come at a better time: the Russian economy grew for eight straight years, and GDP increased by 72% (measured in purchasing power). This growth was supposedly fueled by the 2000s commodities boom, a recovery from the post-Communist depression, and prudent fiscal and economic policies.

After a brief hiatus as prime minister, Putin returned to the Presidency for his third term in 2012 with 64% of the vote, despite widespread accusations of vote-rigging. His previous two stints as a popular and productive President were not to be repeated though, as oil prices fell, and international sanctions were imposed at the beginning of 2014 after Russia's annexation of Crimea and military intervention in Ukraine. This led to the Russian economy shrinking by 3.7% in 2015. A fall in living standards and economic prosperity corresponded with a fall in Putin's popularity.

Hostile military interventions, such as the annexation of Crimea and his support of Syrian tyrant Bashar Al-Assad, has also tarnished his reputation both at home and abroad. Under Putin's leadership, Russia has scored poorly in Transparency International's Corruption Perceptions Index and experienced democratic backsliding according to both the Economist Intelligence Unit's Democracy Index and Freedom House's Freedom in the World index (including a record low 20/100 rating in the 2017 Freedom in the World report, a rating not given since the time of the Soviet Union).

Under Putin's rule, Russia is now no longer seen as a democracy, as is demonstrated through the purging and jailing of political opponents, curtailed press freedom, and the lack of free and fair elections, which confirm that the country is now an autocratic illiberal state.

In 2014, Russia made several military incursions into Ukrainian territory, specifically on the Crimean Peninsula, which was once ruled by the USSR and given to Ukraine in the 1950s as a token of good faith (it was an empty gesture at the time as the USSR essentially owned Ukraine anyway). Since the USSR disbanded, however, Russia wants the area back now as it has become an area of significant strategic importance due to its housing of a naval base and their Black Sea/Mediterranean naval fleet, as well as significant oil and gas pipelines.

These hostilities towards other states that Russia deems in its sphere of influence is particularly concerning for Western states such as the U.S. and the European Union because it represents a new kind of Russian foreign policy. It is essentially a shift from "state-driven foreign policy" to a more offensive strategy, ominously reminiscent of past Soviet regimes, the reunification of which is often thought to be Putin's true vision. At the very least, it represents Putin's attempt at blocking Western influence in the Russian region.

This motive is also made transparent by the Russian military's intervention in the Syrian civil war initiated in September 2015. Military activities in the region consisted of air strikes, cruise missile strikes, and the use of front-line advisors and Russian special forces against militant groups opposed to the Syrian government, following a formal request by the Syrian government for military help against rebel and jihadist groups.

The Middle East and Europe are not the only areas where Putin likes to test the boundaries. In January 2017, a U.S. intelligence community assessment expressed "high confidence" that Putin personally ordered an "influence campaign," initially to denigrate Hillary Clinton and to harm her electoral chances and potential presidency, then later developing "a clear preference" for Donald Trump. Despite Putin's obvious and immediate denial, The New York Times reported in July 2018 that the CIA had long nurtured a Russian source who eventually rose to a position close to Putin, allowing the source to pass key information in 2016 about Putin's direct involvement.

Between the U.S. political quagmire, Brexit, the European Sovereign debt crises as well as the lack of repercussions for his excursions into Ukraine and the Middle East, Putin can only be imagined lying on a bearskin rug in his Saint Petersburg apartment, casually smiling with the knowledge that the West is unravelling whilst Russia continues to push the boundaries seemingly unpunished. Yet his glee seems to be short-lived, for he has problems of his own. In January 2019, the percentage of Russians trusting the president hit a then-historic minimum of 33.4%. His nervousness was revealed by his tactics of intimidation and forceful elimination of his opposition, such as Alexei Navalny, who is Putin's main political competitor. Navalny was arrested numerous times on speculated and unbacked charges, often conveniently before rallies and protests.

The decline is even larger in the 17-25 demographic who find themselves largely disconnected from the country's aging leadership, the nostalgic Soviet rhetoric, and nepotistic agenda. The percentage of people willing to emigrate permanently in this age group is 41%, while 60% have favorable views of the United States (three times more than the 55+ age group). Decline in support for Putin and his illiberal government is also visible in other indicators, such as the public's rapidly growing readiness to protest against poor living conditions, something which would have been unimaginable just a few years ago.

Despite winning his fourth presidential term in 2018, his time is coming to an end. Putin announced that he would not run for president in 2024, as compelled by the Russian Constitution. Many feared he could try to change the term limits, as Xi Jinping managed in China, to try and hold onto power as long as possible. Being a pragmatic man, and realizing his popularity is waning, Putin will most likely cling to power through a less prominent position. Only time will tell if a new political force can break the wall of authoritarianism and pull Russia out of its repressed and restricted state for a thrust into a new democratic era of freedom and prosperity. The rest of the world watches on.

Xi Jinping

Bull in a China Shop

It is not often that one goes from living in a flea-infested cave to becoming the single most powerful man in the world. Yet that is exactly the tale of the current Chinese President Xi Jinping. Ranked according to "Forbes List of the World's Most Powerful People" – based on the amount of human and financial resources that they have sway over and influence on world events – Xi Jinping now sits at the top of the tree of power, above Vladimir Putin in second and Donald Trump in third. This rise comes from a paltry 9th position in 2012 when even Benedict XVI, Pope of the Holy See, outranked him. The key to his success? Well, not having to abide by many rules helps. But his vision for a powerful Communist China and his extreme motivation to achieve it may have started to turn the "Chinese Dream" into a reality.

Xi Jinping's official titles vary wide and far. He is the general secretary of the Communist Party of China (CPC), the President of the People's Republic of China (PRC), and Chairman of the Central Military Commission (CMC). Unofficially, he is often referred to as the "Paramount Leader" of China since his confirmation as president in 2013. Through these great many positions, Xi Jinping has rather successfully centralized his power and created working groups with himself at the helm to subvert and bypass what little government bureaucracy or legislation there was, creating his own destiny as the unmistakable central figure of the new administration. The bypassing of existing institutions through his new "Central Working Groups" allows Xi to create or destroy any policies he deems fit, without fear of opposition. For him, this means fast and efficient policy changes, but for the rest of China, it means having little control or say on how they are governed. He has even used this system to abolish term limits for presidents, allowing himself to govern for as long as he likes.

Since assuming power, Xi Jinping has introduced far-ranging measures to enforce party discipline and to ensure internal unity. In his aim to consolidate power under a communist regime, his primary focus has been on eliminating corruption. This is thought to be the biggest threat to a stable communist state and one of the leading causes of the Arab Spring protests, which plagued much of the Middle East and Africa this past decade. Xi Jinping recognizes the threat that corruption can bring through protests and uprisings. In a bid to stamp this out, he has made his anti-corruption campaign his signature policy, which has resulted in the downfall of many Chinese Party officials and further consolidated his own power.

Perhaps Xi's deepest reform, however, is his far-reaching agenda announced almost immediately after his inauguration as president, alluding to significant changes in both economic and social policy. Termed "comprehensive deepening reforms," they were said to be the most significant since Deng Xiaoping's 1992 "Southern Tour." These reforms aimed to gradually reduce the state's involvement in the distribution of capital and restructure state-owned enterprises to allow further competition, potentially by attracting foreign and private sector players in industries that were previously highly regulated. Xi calls this hybrid mix of capitalism under communist control "capitalism with Chinese characteristics." Judging by Chinese economic growth figures over the last decade, it appears to be working well.

It is not just at home where his influence has increased. He has also championed a more assertive foreign policy, particularly concerning China-Japan relations, China's claims in the South China Sea, and its role as a leading advocate of free trade and globalization.

The dispute over the South China Sea served as a bigger proxy for China's influence in global politics. As early as the 1970s, countries began to claim islands and various zones in the South China Sea, such as the Spratly Islands, which possess rich natural resources (oil and gas) and fishing areas. China claimed that under international law, foreign militaries are not allowed to conduct intelligence-gathering activities, such as reconnaissance flights, in its exclusive economic zone (EEZ). According to the United States and under the UN Convention of the Law of the Sea (UNCLOS), claimant countries should have freedom of navigation through EEZs in the sea and are not required to notify claimants of military activities. In July 2016, the Permanent Court of Arbitration at The Hague issued its ruling on a claim brought against China by the Philippines under UNCLOS, ruling in favor of the Philippines on almost every count. While China is a signatory to the treaty, which established the tribunal, it refuses to accept the court's authority. The resulting standoff further reinforces China's image, proving to the world that it can even take on superpowers such as the U.S.

To further distance itself from Western influence, Xi has cultivated stronger relations with Russia, particularly in the wake of the Ukraine crisis of 2014. He seems to have developed a strong personal relationship with President Vladimir Putin. Both are viewed as strong leaders with a nationalist orientation who are not afraid to assert themselves against Western interests. Xi attended the opening ceremonies of the 2014 Winter Olympics in Sochi. Under Xi, China also signed a $400 billion gas deal with Russia on top of being their largest trading partner.

Having so much power with so little accountability comes at a price, however. For China's 1.4 billion residents, the cost for the public is incredibly limited free speech and autonomy of their own lives. Since Xi became the General Secretary of the CPC, censorship has been "significantly stepped up."

A cryptically named "Document No. 9" is a widely circulated internal & confidential document within the Communist Party of China in 2013. The document warns of seven dangerous Western values: constitutional democracy, universal values of human rights, civil society, pro-market neoliberalism, media independence, historical nihilism (criticisms of past errors), and questioning the nature of Chinese style socialism. In a bid to forcibly prevent any of these dangers to communism surfacing, Xi Jinping has prevented any form of coverage of these topics. A law was also enacted in September 2013, authorizing a three-year prison term for bloggers who shared any content considered "defamatory" more than 500 times.

The persecution extends past just journalists and those who oppose the beliefs of the ruling communist party. Uyghurs (a Muslim minority in Xianjing province) have been suffering in China for many years in one of the most disgusting yet underreported human rights abuses of the world. Under Xianjing's "fully-fledged police state," extensive controls have been placed on their religious, cultural, and social lives. In a bid to stop supposed religious extremism, the Chinese government has expanded police surveillance to monitor even the mildest of acts, such as owning books about Uyghurs, possessing a Muslim prayer rug, and even growing a beard. The government has also installed surveillance cameras in the personal homes of private citizens.

Furthermore, at least 120,000 (and possibly over 1 million according to some estimates) Uyghurs are detained in mass detention camps, termed "re-education camps," aimed at changing the political thinking of detainees, their identities, and their religious beliefs. Make no mistake, these camps are cruel and heavily abuse individual human rights and values. Some of these facilities keep prisoners detained around the clock, while others release their inmates at night to return home. The New York Times has reported that inmates are required to "sing hymns praising the Chinese Communist Party and write 'self-criticism' essays," and that prisoners are also subjected to physical and verbal abuse by prison guards.

The creation of these "mega-prisons," for those who have committed the crime of merely belonging to a Muslim minority, shows the extent Xi Jinping must go to maintain the image of the communist ideal. Even the most innocent of fictional animated characters, 'Winnie-the-Pooh,' was blocked on Chinese social media sites in 2017 following the spread of an internet meme in which photographs of Xi and other individuals were compared to Winnie the Pooh and other characters. As China's economy continues to grow, and the GDP per head increases, a rapidly expanding middle class will bring with it an increasing need for a transparent government and greater individual freedom and rights. Xi will have to maintain control and fight against the rights of his own nation if he is to maintain his forced control of everything. Judging by past events, such as the imprisonment of Uyghurs to control social media, it will not be a fair one.

Nicolas Maduro

Tug of War

The sheer scale of Nicolas Maduro's failures knows no bounds. Having occupied the Venezuelan presidency since 2013, he has almost single-handedly driven Venezuela and its 32 million inhabitants to the brink of despair. At the time of writing, his presidency is in dispute, having been accused by over 50 countries of rigging a sham election in 2019. Yet his brutal reign still continues in some capacity, even as most of Venezuela and many other countries, such as Canada, the U.S., and the UK, recognize Juan Guaido as the legitimate successor after Maduro's public ousting.

Maduro has managed to cling on to some form of power thanks to his predecessor, Hugo Chavez, who systematically weakened all the main institutions in the country, stacking everything in the ruling party's favor and ensured opposition-led change would be challenging or impossible. Maduro's cronies placed in almost all of these false institutions allowed him to remain within the political radar, despite being declared illegitimate by the only remaining independent institution, the National Assembly.

The road to Maduro's downfall is a familiar story to that of many failed presidencies. Food shortages in Venezuela and decreased living standards led to protests beginning in 2014 that escalated into daily marches nationwide, repression of dissent, and a decline in Maduro's popularity. According to The New York Times, Maduro's administration was held responsible for "grossly mis-managing the economy and plunging the country into a deep humanitarian crisis" and attempting to "crush the opposition by jailing or exiling critics and using lethal force against anti-government protesters."

Maduro has been described by many as a "dictator," and an Organization of American States (OAS) report determined that numerous crimes against humanity have been committed during his presidency. Under Maduro's regime, an estimated 9,000+ people were executed for "resistance to authority," and more than 4 million forced to flee. Maduro's allies, including China, Cuba, Russia, Iran, and Turkey, denounce what they call "interference in Venezuela's domestic affairs." AP News reported that "familiar geopolitical sides" had formed in the 2019 Venezuelan presidential crisis, with allies Russia, China, Iran, Syria, and Cuba supporting Maduro, and the US., Canada, and most of Western Europe supporting Guaidó as interim president. Figure 6 shows the split in global support for Maduro's tyrannical government with a clear east-west divide.

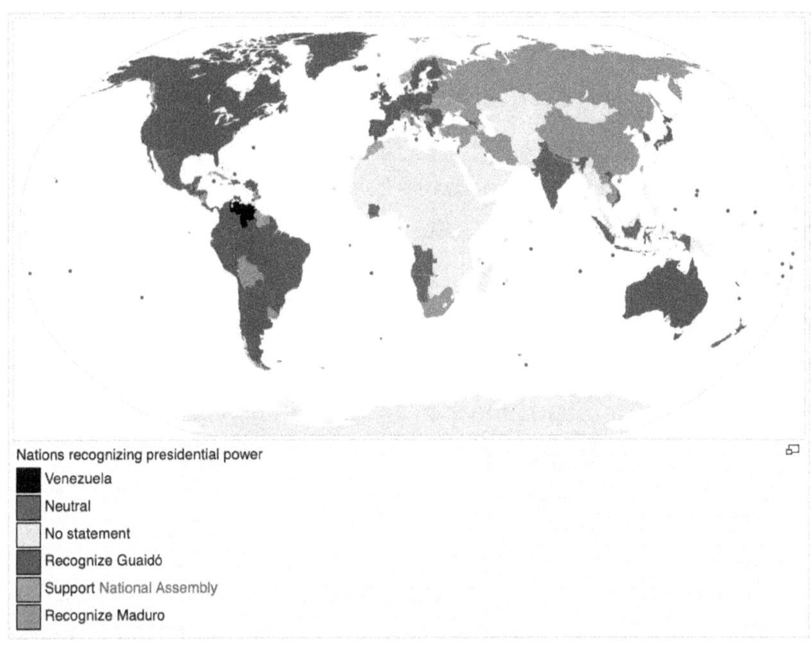

Figure 6: Global divide over Venezuela's legitimate leader

Amid widespread condemnation and illegitimacy, President Maduro was sworn in on 10 January 2019. Just 13 days later, amid mass protests and a military coup, the president of the National Assembly, Guaidó, was declared the interim president. Maduro's government states that the crisis is a "coup d'état" led by the United States to topple him and control the country's oil reserves. Guaidó denies the coup allegations, saying peaceful volunteers back his movement.

This is only the tip of the iceberg of Maduro's criminal record. Two nephews of Maduro's wife, Efraín Antonio Campo Flores and Francisco Flores de Freitas, were found guilty in a U.S. court of conspiracy to import cocaine in November 2016. It might have been conceivable that some of their funds assisted Maduro's presidential campaign in both the 2013 and 2015 elections.

His party's corruption perpetually keeps the people of his country hungry. An April 2019 communication from the United States Department of State highlighted a 2017 National Assembly investigation finding that the government paid US$42 for food that cost under US$13, and that "Maduro's inner circle kept the difference, which totaled more than $200 million dollars in at least one case", adding that food boxes were "distributed in exchange for votes" among the public.

Whilst in exile in 2018, Maduro was sentenced to 18 years of imprisonment by the Supreme Tribunal of Justice of Venezuela for corruption charges after receiving $35 million from the construction company Odebrecht in exchange for prioritized construction projects in Venezuela.

The results of his mismanagement and corruption are extreme for Venezuela. Hyperinflation reached over 1,000,000% at its peak, and there have been drastic increases in rates of unemployment, poverty, disease, child mortality, malnutrition, and crime. These factors have precipitated the Venezuelan migrant crisis, where more than three million people have fled the country. The fact that such an incompetent president cannot be officially ousted divulges the scale of the infectious corruption that still holds Maduro to power. The battle between Juan Guaido and his supporters (the West) and Nicolas Maduro and his supporters (the East) continues on, but the conclusion will be hugely important to South America. Should his illegitimate presidency return to official power, the dictatorship will discourage democracy in the area and likely lead to more turmoil. Only time can tell whether justice will prevail.

Mohammad Bin Salman

Saint or Sinner?

If Xi Jinping takes the trophy for the quickest rise to power, then Mohammad Bin Salman (or MBS as he is colloquially known), Saudi Arabia's Crown Prince, comes in a close second. Mohammad currently serves as the deputy prime minister under the power of the prime minister held by King Salman bin Abdulaziz Al Saud. Like Xi Jinping, he reigns over many other institutions; he is chairman of the Council for Economic and Development Affairs, chairman of the Council of Political and Security Affairs, and Minister of Defense. The biggest revelation is his age at the time of his appointment - as of 2019, he is only 33 years old.

Despite being under the lead of the King, he has been described as the true official behind the power, calling all the shots. He was appointed crown prince in June 2017, following King Salman's decision to remove Muhammad bin Nayef from all positions and thereby making Mohammed bin Salman heir presumptive to the throne. His power has been bolstered through newfound allies across the world, especially in the U.S., with Trump having called the Prince on the day of his anointing to "congratulate him on his new elevation." According to the White House, Trump and the new crown prince pledged "close cooperation" on security and economic issues. Both leaders also discussed the need to cut off support for terrorism, the recent diplomatic dispute with Qatar, and the push to secure peace between Israel and the Palestinians. Mohammed bin Salman told the Washington Post in April 2017 that without America's cultural influence on Saudi Arabia, "we would have ended up like North Korea."

Perhaps the most notable, and in theory, laudable policy of his recent elevation is the liberalization of a country, which has, for decades, been subject to extremely tight and restrictive laws based around extreme Muslim practices. MBS is said to have recognized the failure of previous Saudi states due to familial infighting, inherent corruption, and a failure to modernize. His reform started with a heavy and forceful attack on corruption.

In May 2017, Mohammed bin Salman publicly warned, "I confirm to you, no one will survive in a corruption case—whoever he is, even if he's a prince or a minister." Following this, he ordered some 200 wealthy businessmen and princes to be placed under house arrest in Riyadh's Ritz Carlton hotel in November 2017. Since then, over 40 princes and government ministers have been arrested on corruption and money laundering charges. This purge on corruption seems to be popular with the large majority of Arab youth, with a 2018 survey showing nine out of ten 18 to 24-year-olds in the MENA region (Middle East and North Africa) support MBS's crusade against corruption.

While this purge against corruption is a noble effort, the true intention behind his campaign is thought to lie in another direction. One hypothesis indicates that the arrests were part of a power grab on the part of Prince. The New York Times wrote: "The sweeping campaign of arrests appears to be the latest move to consolidate the power of Crown Prince Mohammed bin Salman, the favorite son and top adviser of King Salman. The king had decreed the creation of a powerful new anti-corruption committee, headed by the crown prince, only hours before the committee ordered the arrests." Robert Jordan, the former U.S. ambassador to Saudi Arabia, also said that: "I would say it's a classical power grab move sometimes to arrest your rivals and your potential rivals under the pretext of corruption."

Whatever the intention, there is no doubt that life for ordinary citizens of the kingdom has improved, especially for women whose rights have previously been heavily restricted. He has led several successful reforms, which include regulations restricting the powers of the religious police, the removal of the ban on female drivers in June 2018, and the weakening of the male-guardianship system in August 2019. Seeking to modernize the country, Saudi Arabia has seen the first Saudi public concert by a female singer, the first Saudi sports stadium to admit women, an increased presence of women in the workforce, and an invitation for international tourists to visit the country through an e-visa system which can now easily issue visas over the internet so that travelers can attend special events and festivals.

Perhaps his most ambitious reform, however, is in his "Vision 2030" program. This aims to address one of the greatest economic concerns of the country, which is its over-dependence on oil. MBS plans to diversify the country's finances through investment in non-oil related industries, including technology and tourism. In 2016, in an unprecedented motion, he announced plans to list the shares of the state oil company Saudi Aramco, a petroleum behemoth estimated as between $1.7 - $2.3 trillion dollars, with just a 2-5% share estimated to raise up to $115 billion.

Other plans to branch out from its overdependence on oil are just as extreme. In October 2017, bin Salman announced plans for the creation of Neom, a $500 billion economic zone to cover an area of 26,000 square kilometers on Saudi Arabia's Red Sea coast, extending into Jordan and Egypt. Neom aims to attract investment in sectors, including renewable energy, biotechnology, robotics, and advanced manufacturing. Even more remarkably, plans call for the city to be powered entirely by renewable energy, with wireless hi-speed internet free to all. All services and processes in NEOM are planned to be 100% fully automated, with the goal of becoming the most efficient and modern destination in the world. Whilst this may sound a little overzealous, it reveals the thinking and direction behind MBS and his new vision for Saudi Arabia.

Whilst this may all sound commendable, if not a little optimistic, delving deeper into the politics of the new system shows a much darker system. Despite praise for his strides towards the social and economic liberalization of Saudi Arabia, international commentators and human rights groups have been vocally critical of bin Salman's leadership and the shortfalls of his reform program, citing a rising number of detentions and alleged torture of human rights activists. He has also been accused of a bombing campaign in Yemen, resulting in war-induced famine and has caused an estimated 13 million civilians to starve. Other offences include the escalation of the Qatar diplomatic crisis, the start of the Lebanon–Saudi Arabia dispute, the start of a diplomatic spat with Canada, the 2018–2019 Saudi crackdown on feminists. He has been described by observers as an autocratic leader, with no tolerance for dissidence against him or the Saudi royal family. He has even reportedly created the "Tiger Squad," a team of assassins that act as a death squad.

The most notable alleged victim of this "private hit squad" was Saudi journalist Jamal Khashoggi, a known and outspoken critic of the crown prince. In 2018, Jamal went missing after entering the Saudi consulate in Istanbul. Turkish officials reportedly believe that Khashoggi was murdered at the consulate, claiming to have specific video and audio recordings proving that Khashoggi was first tortured and then murdered and that a medical forensics expert was part of the 15-man Saudi team seen entering and leaving the consulate at the time of the journalist's disappearance, seven of which are members of Mohammed bin Salman's personal bodyguards. Despite obvious claims by the crown prince of his lack of involvement, multiple analyses of the event by agencies including the British MI6 and the U.S. CIA have all concluded that in the presence of all known evidence, it is very likely that Mohammed bin Salman ordered the killing of Khashoggi. Even Donald Trump, a previous ally and confidant, described the Saudi response to the killing as "one of the worst in the history of cover-ups." The brutal murder of Khashoggi was thought to have been motivated by the Prince's privately stated belief that Khashoggi was an Islamist with problematic connections to the Muslim Brotherhood, a perception that differs markedly from the Saudi government's public remarks on Khashoggi's death.

Prince Mohammad's rise to power in one of the most influential Arabic states has been a mixed blessing for both Saudi Arabia and international politics in general. If he succeeds in his modernization efforts, Saudis will benefit from new opportunities and freedoms, and the world will benefit from the curtailing of radical religious agendas. In the not too distant future, the kingdom could look more like the United Arab Emirates, its prosperous and relatively forward-looking neighbor. However, the way MBS executed these ideas and practiced extreme suppression of his critics are unworthy of praise and risks drowning the country in criticisms and sanctions from the rest of the world. Whilst his vision is looking mainly to the future, his authoritarian methods of control are old fashioned, and he risks becoming the very thing he swore to eradicate.

2. Business & Economics

Sharing Economy

Sharing is Caring

In an ironic twist of fate, the increasing use of technology and the internet has brought us closer to times more familiar in the past; where economies were smaller scale, more localized and relied on sole traders as opposed to the mammoth corporations of late, where supermarkets are more familiar than market stalls. The sharing economy, however, is a signifier of the future economy retrograding to past practices.

The sharing economy, or shareconomy, is a term used to describe a way of distributing goods and services, which differs from the traditional model of corporations hiring employees to sell products to consumers. In the sharing economy, individuals are said to rent or "share" things such as their cars, homes, and personal time to other individuals in a peer-to-peer fashion. This is mostly accessed through community-based online platforms, and increasingly from apps on smartphones and tablets. As long as a smartphone is at arm's length, access to millions of buyers and sellers is merely a tap away.

The attraction of this for most users is the ability to turn their unused and often costly assets into income. Idle assets such as cars, spare bedrooms, and even labor can be rented out to the highest bidder, often at more appealing prices to both buyer and seller than those of traditional corporations. Car sharing services, such as Zipcar, best illustrate this idea. Data provided by the Brookings Institute shows private vehicles remain unused for 95% of their lifetime, sitting idle in parking lots or on the drive. Yet, owners still bear the costs for this in terms of ownership and depreciation. The same report detailed the room-sharing service Airbnb's cost advantage over hotel space as homeowners make use of spare bedrooms. Airbnb rates were reported to be between 30-60% cheaper than hotel rates around the world, where corporate structures and legalities increase prices compared to small scale rentals.

The 2010s witnessed a large-scale expansion of sharing economy services in four particular subcategories:

1) Co-working Platforms - Companies that provide shared open workspaces for freelancers, entrepreneurs, and work-from-home employees in major metropolitan areas. WeWork, appraised as the sixth-largest private startup in the world, is the most popular coworking company by far, with over 160 locations in 16 countries.

2) Peer-to-Peer Lending Platforms - Companies that allow individuals to lend money to other individuals at rates cheaper than those offered through traditional credit lending entities. Upstart is the current dominant player in this market, offering loans starting from a minimum of $1,000 to a maximum of $50,000 at an annual percentage rate (APR) starting at 8.85%.

3) Fashion Platforms - Sites allowing individuals to sell or rent their clothes. Whilst the idea of borrowing another's clothes may repulse some, clothing rental is a rapidly increasing industry. It avoids the

waste involved in buying special occasion clothing and wearing it infrequently.

4) Freelancing Platforms - Sites that offer to match freelance workers across a wide spectrum ranging from traditional freelance work to services traditionally reserved for handymen. Fiverr, Upwork, and Freelancer.com have seen both buyers and sellers in this field increase exponentially.

The sharing economy's explosive growth has astounded even the most optimistic market pundits. From just a few at the start of the 2010s, there are now thousands of sharing economy platforms operating across countless industries globally. Back in 2009, there were only a handful of platforms available: Zipcar, BlaBlaCar, and Couchsurfing were the dominant few. Airbnb launched in Fall 2008, and Uber followed suit in Spring 2009. Together, these two 'shareconomy' behemoths have spurred much of this peer-to-peer growth.

The sharing economy is often referred to as the "access economy "due to the way it allows users to have quick access to almost all amenities. Access over ownership is a shift that has now firmly taken root, as digital and mobile technologies make it even easier to access goods and services on-demand. Ownership of cars is now decreasing in most major cities due to the convenience offered by the likes of Uber and Lyft. The combined higher costs of owning and storing a vehicle in town starts to tilt this balance towards a service-on-demand model. It is no longer just a millennial preference, but a societal one as well.

On the eve of its next decade, what can be expected of the sharing economy? Forecasts predict growth from $14 billion in 2014 to $335 billion by 2025. We can expect to see more companies following in Uber's and Airbnb's footsteps, offering large IPOs, as competition forces companies to raise cash fast by going public. Uber and Lyft both went public in 2019, with valuations of $58 billion and $16 billion, respectively. Airbnb is expected to join this club of public unicorns with an expected IPO in 2020, valuing the company around $30-$35 billion.

It hasn't all been plain-sailing for these companies, however. The sheer speed of the shareconomy growth has far outpaced governance and regulatory oversight of it. A lack of regulation has already led to serious abuses to both buyers and sellers. This has been highlighted through numerous highly publicized cases involving hidden cameras in rented rooms, lawsuits over unfair treatment of ride-sharing contractors by the platforms that employ them, and even murders of customers by real or fraudulent rental and ride-share providers. These concerns have diminished the apeal of the sharing economy on the general public, as shown in Figure 7 based on data by PwC analysis.

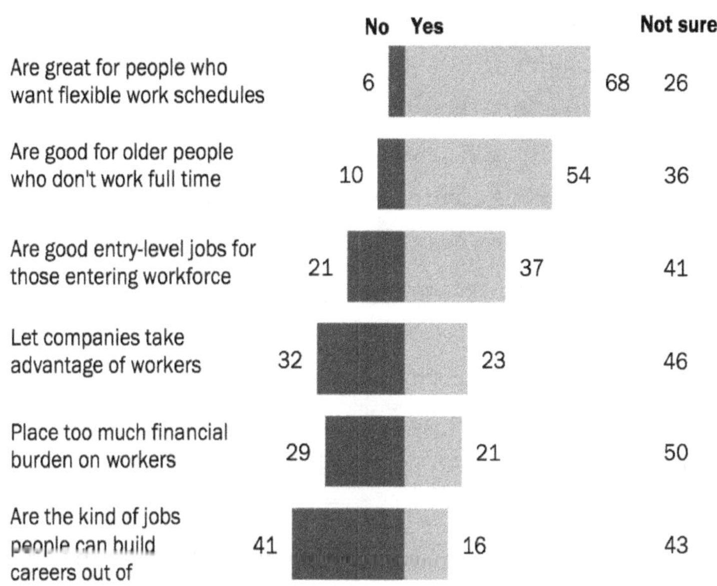

Figure 7: American's mixed views on internet-enabled gig work.

Uber, in particular, has been besieged by such issues. The most prominent, and still ongoing case involves the employment status of its workers and whether they should be treated as independent contractors or employees. These two types of workers are treated very differently; contract workers are generally not guaranteed any benefits, and pay can be below average. Employees, however, are granted access to benefits, and pay is generally higher. Unsurprisingly, their platforms are keen to maintain the status of their workers as contractors as they are both cheaper and easier to hire and fire. This debate had prompted Uber to remove their presence in several locations such as Alaska, where a large controversy arose when Uber drivers were registered as taxi drivers, entitling them to workers' compensation insurance. However, if they were considered independent contractors, they would not receive these same benefits. Due to all of the disputes, Uber pulled services from Alaska. Also, ride-share drivers' status continues to be ambiguous when it comes to legal matters. On New Year's Eve in 2013, an off-duty driver for Uber killed a pedestrian while looking for a rider. Since the driver was considered a contractor, Uber would not compensate the victim's family. Uber's contract states that the service is a matching platform, and "the company does not provide transportation services, and … has no liability for services... provided by third parties."

A stagnant economic climate has also been a key driver for the growth of the sharing economy. New York Magazine wrote that the sharing economy has succeeded at large partly because the real economy has been struggling. Specifically, in the magazine's view, the sharing economy succeeds because of a depressed labor market, in which "lots of people are trying to fill holes in their income by monetizing their stuff and their labor in creative ways." In many cases, people join the sharing economy because they've recently lost a full-time job, including some instances where the pricing structure of the sharing economy may have made their old jobs less profitable (e.g. full-time taxi drivers who may have switched to Lyft or Uber). The magazine writes that "In almost every case, what compels people to open up their homes and cars to complete strangers is money, not trust. … Tools that help people trust in the kindness of strangers might be pushing hesitant sharing-economy participants over the threshold to adoption. But what's getting them to the threshold in the first place is a damaged economy and harmful public policy that has forced millions of people to look to odd jobs for sustenance."

It is still relatively early days for the sharing economy, and many of these kinks will be ironed out as these companies mature, and government regulation becomes thorough and consistent. Until then, we will see continued growth in this industry, with new companies entering and exiting the market where untrodden avenues are explored. There will undoubtedly be more backlash between companies and governments as the battle between cash and regulation rages on, as most recently witnessed by current tech giants such as Facebook and Google.

E-commerce

Happy Hour

Macy's, American Apparel, GAP, Toys R Us and Victoria's Secret. These are just a handful of once-prosperous retailers who failed to see the explosive growth of e-commerce (electronic commerce). The "Retail Apocalypse," as it is often referred to, has conceived the demise of some of the largest names in the retail industry. Whilst e-commerce has been ramping up since the beginning of the millennia, this past decade has cemented its rise and continued to dominate how people purchase goods.

Today, this trend shows no signs of abating. An early analysis from Internet Retailer, the leading source for e-commerce news, showed online retail sales in the U.S. alone crossed $517 billion in 2018, which is a 15.0% jump compared to 2017. In contrast, the growth in retail sales at physical stores only reached just 3.7% last year. This means that e-commerce now accounts for 14.3% of total retail sales when factoring out the sale of items not normally purchased online, such as fuel, automobiles, and restaurant spending. It also unveils that in just a decade, the internet has more than doubled its share of retail sales. Ten short years ago, e-commerce was at 5.1% of total retail purchases.

This phenomenon is not restricted to just the U.S. alone. In 2017, retail e-commerce sales across the world reached $2.3 trillion, a 24.8% increase over 2016. Among emerging economies, China's e-commerce presence continues to expand year on year. With 668 million internet users, China's online shopping sales reached $253 billion in the first half of 2015, accounting for 10% of total Chinese consumer retail sales in that period. China is also the largest e-commerce market in the world, with the value of sales at an estimated $899 billion in 2016.

The United Kingdom is currently the most active online-shopping nation, with an average e-commerce spend per capita of $4,201. This is followed by the U.S. and fellow tech lover South Korea with per capita expenditures of $3,428 and $2,591, respectively. Yet when accounting for variances in salary, it is Chinese who collectively spends the most who 19.34% of their salary spent online and followed closely by Mexicans. Interestingly, South Africans are the thriftiest online, spending $171 per capita only, which also equates to the lowest proportion of salary spent at a measly 1.04%.

The main driver of this growth is a shifting technological landscape. Over the past decade, the evolution of both tech hardware and the internet has had a direct correlation with e-commerce. Just as the internet has grown into the desired medium for marketing, advertising, and purchasing of products, goods, and services, e-commerce has grown to traditional rival shopping in many ways. Three key trends have contributed to the rapid growth of e-commerce over the last decade.

The first of these trends is the rise in online marketplaces. Amazon, the undisputed king of e-commerce, has set the consumer benchmark for online shopping. With a huge range of products and the option for next-day and often free delivery, coupled with reasonably lower prices, it appears to be a no-brainer for most shoppers to choose Amazon. Why spend hours physically travelling to town, hoping that a store has what you are looking for, then having to pay full retail price for an unknown brand of which you have no way of knowing the quality?

This problem is mitigated for online shoppers who can now compare prices, brands, read customer reviews, and often purchase products for prices below retail. While this isn't optimal for every purchase, particularly larger and more expensive items such as furniture (which is recommended to be viewed in person), most everyday smaller items are simply more convenient to purchase online. The cut-throat prices that e-commerce can provide are facilitated by a reduction in many overheads for the seller, especially in terms of the lack of need for owning or leasing retail space and the associated costs with occupying the space. Online shops also can be said to have less intense competition from many sellers.

The second key factor is the seamless shift to using mobile devices for online shopping. Mobile shopping, or m-commerce, now represents a vast majority of shoppers who prefer to browse from simple and easy to use apps, which link card payment methods for swifter purchasing. In 2017, m-commerce sales accounted for 34.5% of total e-commerce sales. By 2021, m-commerce sales are expected to account for over half of total e-commerce sales.

The ubiquity of mobile devices is also a primer for the third key factor in the growth of e-commerce; the tremendous surge in online marketing and advertising. Most individuals, particularly the younger demographic, keep their mobile devices close at hand, making them much more accessible to marketers and advertisers. The closer these marketers are to their customers, the more aggressive they can be in pushing sales. Push notifications – instant messages that can reach audiences anywhere and anytime – are an advantage that mobile shopping apps have in re-engaging their customers and promoting sales, usually through offering instant deals.

The main draw for advertisers is that costs and efforts required for push-message advertising are significantly lower than using traditional advertising. Businesses can also now engage with potential customers via a whole host of mediums such as websites, emails, and social media in addition to their physical stores. This creates multiple channels of purchase, receipt, and exchange of goods, with a prevalence of attractive customer service focusing on shopper-friendly shipping and return policies. Customers can purchase online, pick their purchases up at a physical store, return any defective items online, and apply discounts or offers based on a certain number of referrals. This integrated online and physical experience drives further sales.

The burgeoning of e-commerce shows no signs of slowing, as further technological improvements to both hardware and software continue to open more avenues for potential shoppers. Virtual reality (VR) and augmented reality (AR) are only just starting to find applied commercial purposes but have the potential to drive further online sales growth. In a partnership with Australian retailer Myer, eBay has launched the first virtual reality department store. Shoppers can now look through thousands of Myer products through VR headsets. Upon entering the virtual store, various shopping categories are presented, and users can move through virtual "aisles," selecting or rejecting items. The top 100 products are now viewable in 3D, with the remaining 12,500 available in 2D. Instead of having hand controllers, users select items using only sight. The company has coined the term "eBay Sight Search," which allows items to be chosen by simply holding your gaze on a product for a few seconds. This is one of the earliest iterations of online shopping through VR, and as the technology matures and becomes more mainstream, further practical uses will be available for online shoppers.

Innovations like these are why e-commerce sales are predicted to increase in the foreseeable future. Developing countries such as India and much of Asia stand to gain the most as the now pervasive smartphone, combined with rapidly improving delivery services, will create great opportunities. Whether traditional brick-and-mortar stores can survive the e-commerce onslaught remains to be seen, but most will need to create some form of digital presence if they are to survive. As for us consumers, we can expect a much greater quality and quantity of shopping experiences, as online competition and ease of access drives down prices. This is truly a win-win situation.

Western Low Inflation

Of Little Interest

For much of the Western World, the past decade has been excellent for those who borrowed money. Low-interest rates, from the aftermath of the 2007 financial crisis, have yet to return anywhere near their pre-crisis levels, much to the benefit of house-buyers and loan-borrowers. Fiscal policies of low-interest rates and low inflation were only supposed to be a temporary measure to boost spending and jumpstart the economy into recovery, yet here we are over a decade later unable to budge from these low rates. Economists of the world are scratching their heads as to when interest rates will pick up again, while they worry about how long these eerily low rates can be sustained for.

Western economies, such as much of Europe, the U.S., and the UK, have generally recovered well from the infamous 2008 financial crisis. In America, Britain, and Germany, the unemployment rate has crept below 4%, the lowest rate in many decades. Jobs are plentiful and wages are finally starting to rise after years of stagnation, albeit marginally. Tight labor markets are usually an indicator of a healthy economy and, thus, a rising demand for goods and services. To satisfy such a demand, businesses usually raise prices. Yet, despite this growth in demand, inflation has held remarkably steady, contrary to what popular economics dictates.

This has led to paltry savings rates for many individuals. In 2005, the national average U.S. rate on savings accounts was a miserable 0.1%, and in 2009, little has changed as the rate is still below a paltry 0.3%. At the turn of the millennia, just 20 years ago, the rate was 1.73%. Figure 8 shows the slow and steady trend in decreasing interest rates in the U.S., U.K., and Germany. With Germany dipping into the negatives, and the U.K. and U.S. hovering dangerously close to the 0% mark, there is little room to weather future financial storms.

Figure 8: Interest rates in the U.K., U.S., and Germany over time.

As if poor rates on savings were not bad enough, saving for retirement seems just as dismal. Pension funds, overseeing trillions in retirees' future cash, have been ratcheting down return expectations. The 30-year Treasury bond, favored debt security, currently yields only about 2.5%, which pales in comparison to an average of 6.5% since the 1970s. Even a record rise in stock prices hasn't solved the low-return problem for pension funds after most cut their allocations to equities post the financial crisis. Ben Meng, a chief investment officer of the

California Public Employees' Retirement System, said in June that the expected return for his pension portfolio over the next 10 years would be 6.1%, down from a previous target of 7%.

On the plus side, the economic climate has made some purchases more attractive. Thirty-year mortgage rates are a fraction of long-run averages, and businesses too are paying very little to borrow. This has resulted in exactly what the fiscal policies intended to do, which is to spur investment and consumer spending. Homeowners are able to afford relatively affordable mortgage payments or vehicle leases, and entrepreneurs have easy access to cheap money to start or expand their operations. All this cheap money has been helping the economy tick along, contributing to the tight labor market witnessed today.

One might wonder why this is such a bad thing? Why strive for higher interest rates when employment is at its peak, and businesses have better access to cash, which in turn will create investments, jobs, and further opportunities? Whilst short term stimulus has been beneficial for many, long term prospects are much riskier.

One major implication of sustained low-interest rates is the restriction of one of the most powerful tools available for fighting economic recessions and slowdowns. With current interest rates in the U.S. at a mere 1.75%-2%, there is insufficient room to drop interest rates to a significant enough degree to spur economic activity, as was seen in the last recession, where rates dropped by around 5%.

The Federal Reserve had tried to push the U.S. into a higher-rate regime, raising rates nine times since 2015, when the key short-term rate was near zero, in a bid to create this interest rate buffer. Then interest rates began to plunge in parallel with rates in other developed economies such as Germany and Japan. Clearly, some big market participants were anticipating slower growth, especially in the face of the U.S.-China trade war and a generally lagging Eurozone economy. In September 2019, Federal Reserve Chairman Jerome Powell announced that the 'Fed' would cut interest rates for a second time this year to between 1.75% and 2% for fear of a slowing global economy.

As you may have guessed, the U.S. is not the only country experiencing this issue. Depressed U.S. rates come as other central banks, including the European Central Bank (ECB), have turned more dovish and dropped interest rates into the negatives. This period of low European interest stems from the European Sovereign Debt Crisis of 2011, where the European currency was on the brink of collapse. In a bid to achieve its 2% inflation target, the ECB introduced negative interest rates in June 2014, lowering its deposit rate to -0.1% in an attempt to stimulate the economy. Describing the Eurozone economy as mired in a period of "protracted" weakness, ECB chief Mario Draghi announced further cuts in September 2019 to -0.5%, meaning savers have to pay 0.5% of their savings simply to keep their money in a bank.

Despite the U.S. Federal Reserve aiming to minimize further reductions in interest rates, it appears President Donald Trump has other ideas. The president tweeted that Federal officials should slash interest rates to zero or below. In doing so, he urged the central bank to adopt a policy that its counterparts, including the European

Central Bank and Bank of Japan, have used as an emergency measure to shore up weak economies. Aside from reduced borrowing costs, negative rates help weaken a country's currency by making it a less attractive investment than other currencies. Intentionally weakening a currency gives exports a competitive advantage and boosts inflation by pushing up import costs. This is one of Trump's motivations for wanting negative rates on the dollar. Negative central bank rates also lower borrowing costs on a whole range of instruments meaning that businesses and households get even cheaper loans.

Whether low or even negative, it is clear that interest rates will remain suppressed for the foreseeable future. As much as this should boost consumer spending and economic confidence, global risks that are beyond any country's control (such as a weak Europe and U.S.-China trade tariffs) bring about a fear of global economic decline. For the next recession, it will be a matter of 'when' and not 'if.' It will be much harder to fight when interest rates are already rock bottom and cannot be manipulated further. This means other controversial methods will need to be employed, such as more quantitative easing. Until then, individuals should make the most of cheap loans while they can.

European Sovereign Debt Crisis

Spread Like Wildfire

If there is one place you would think money would be safe, it would be a bank. Yet this couldn't have been any further from the truth, especially for Greece in 2015. Greek banks completely shut down for 20 days and prohibited anyone from withdrawing any cash for weeks. Parents fretted, and pensioners were left without access to vital funds. Only in September 2015 were all restrictions on withdrawing cash in Greece fully removed, but the lingering effects felt by Greece's 10 million citizens still remains.

Greece, along with a handful of other fiscally weak European states, has been crippled by extreme debt and depressing austerity measures throughout the entirety of the past decade. This debt crisis experienced in European states such as Portugal, Ireland, Greece, and Spain, all part of what is termed the European sovereign-debt crisis. This event traces its roots back to the 2008 financial crisis, which acted as a trigger in an already loaded deadly weapon of debt.

During this period, several European countries experienced the collapse of financial institutions, high government debt, and rapidly rising bond yield spreads in government securities. Iceland's banking system was the first to fall in 2008, following the default of all three of its major privately-owned commercial banks. Relative to the size of its economy, Iceland's systemic banking collapse was the largest experienced by any country's economy in history. The shockwaves spread to other economically weak countries, including Portugal,

Italy, Ireland, Greece, and Spain, in 2009. The speed, scale, and intensity of these failures lead to a damaging loss of confidence in European businesses and economies as a whole, affecting almost every other European country.

As with most economic catastrophes, the root cause of this event was uncontrolled debt. A country's total national debt can be thought of as the sum of its internal and external debt, with external debt referred to as sovereign debt. This sovereign debt relates to the bonds issued by a nation's government in a foreign currency, which is then sold to foreign investors. Whereas internal debt can more easily be paid off, by raising taxes or printing more money, these tactics cannot be applied to sovereign debt, as you cannot print another country's currency. As the financial crisis hit and governments suddenly found themselves unable to pay their sovereign debts, many were suddenly exposed to monetary default. Some countries, especially Greece, who was already in a financial tight spot, were particularly vulnerable. Its missed payment of €1.6 billion in 2015 to the International Monetary Fund (IMF) signaled for the first time in history a developed nation had missed such a payment, sparking fear in other countries who were in similarly risky positions.

Being unable to pay its debts and on the brink of bankruptcy, Greece needed swift major help. Bailouts from the IMF and other European creditors were granted, but on the condition of strict budget reforms, namely cuts to spending and increasing tax revenues. These austerity measures crippled productivity in Greece and created a vicious cycle of recession, with unemployment reaching 25.4% in August 2012. Not only did this decrease tax revenues, worsening Greece's fiscal position, but it also created a humanitarian crisis. Homelessness increased, suicides hit record highs, and public health significantly deteriorated. Such severe austerity measures, amidst the worst financial crisis since the Great Depression, proved to be one of the largest factors contributing to this economic implosion.

It wasn't long until Ireland followed Greece in requiring a bailout in November 2010, with Portugal following in May 2011. Spain, Italy, and Cyprus also required official assistance in June 2012. The crisis was still continuing mid-way into the decade when a combination of market volatility triggered by 'Brexit,' questionable politicians, and a poorly managed financial system worsened the situation for Italian banks in mid-2016. A staggering 17% of Italian loans, approximately $400 billion-worth, were rendered junk with banks needing significant bailouts.

The crisis was eventually controlled by the financial guarantees of European countries and by the IMF, who feared the collapse of the euro. The European Stability Mechanism (ESM) was eventually created as a permanent rescue funding program, entering into force in 2012. Such a program serves as a 'financial firewall,' preventing the default of one country from rippling through the entire interconnected financial system. This firewall mechanism ensures that downstream nations and banking systems are protected by guaranteeing some or all of their obligations, thus managing the single default while limiting financial contagion.

Although the worst is certainly over, the lingering austerity effects are still felt in some European states. Greece's economy is still highly uncertain, with an unemployment rate of approximately 21%. Italy fell back into a recession in the last half of 2018, for the third time in a decade. The UK is on the cusp of financial disaster as a hard 'Brexit' looks increasingly unavoidable. With an overarching gloom over the economic outlook, along with U.S.-China trade wars and finally worryingly little productivity growth, the economic environment does not seem ready for recovery. At least Europe, thanks to a relatively strong Germany and a stable France, is starting to understand its importance as a source of security amid the unpredictable U.S., boosting confidence in the region. The worst already looks to be over, but the next decade will be crucial for maintaining the recovery and sustaining future growth.

Wealth Inequality

What's Yours Is Mine

At its peak, the Roman Empire encompassed an incredible five million square kilometers of land by 117 AD. As a result of its mammoth sphere of influence, Ancient Rome created extraordinary wealth for those elites in control. Marcus Licinius Crassus was certainly one of them, having often been listed among the "wealthiest individuals in history. Depending on the estimate of the adjusted value of a Roman sesterce, his net worth has been placed in the range of US$200 million to US$20 billion in modern terms, with much of this wealth derived from the trading of slaves.

One would think that in modern times, it has become easier to spread wealth. With access to modern technology, global markets, and education, todays poorest at least have some access to wealth-building tools. Yet incredibly, the Romans, even with their propensity for using slave labor, created an economy with less income inequality than the current flagship superpower, the U.S. Income inequality throughout much of the Western world has widened this past decade, much to the displeasure of the middle classes who have been further squeezed by a decade of austerity.

Definitions can vary, but income inequality concerns the unequal distribution of income and opportunity between different groups in society, such as the wealthy having a disproportionately large amount of capital compared to middle and lower classes. It is a concern in almost all countries around the world and often traps people in poverty with little chance to climb up the social ladder. What's worse is that the vicious cycle created by owning vast wealth – thanks to the power of compound interest – makes large sums of money grow exponentially.

The statistics unveil the true scale of the imbalance. In the U.S., the supposed standard of democracy, the top 10% of earners now average more than nine times as much income as the bottom 90 percent. Americans in the top 1%, however, average over 39 times more income than the bottom 90%. That means one in 100 Americans earns almost as much in one single year than 10% of hardworking Americans earn throughout their entire life. But even that gap pales in comparison to the divide between the nation's top 0.1% and everyone else. Americans at this tier are earning over 188 times the income of the bottom 90%. Figure 9 shows the growth of after-tax income between the top 1% and bottom 20% prior to 2017. The trend here clearly denotes a widening gap.

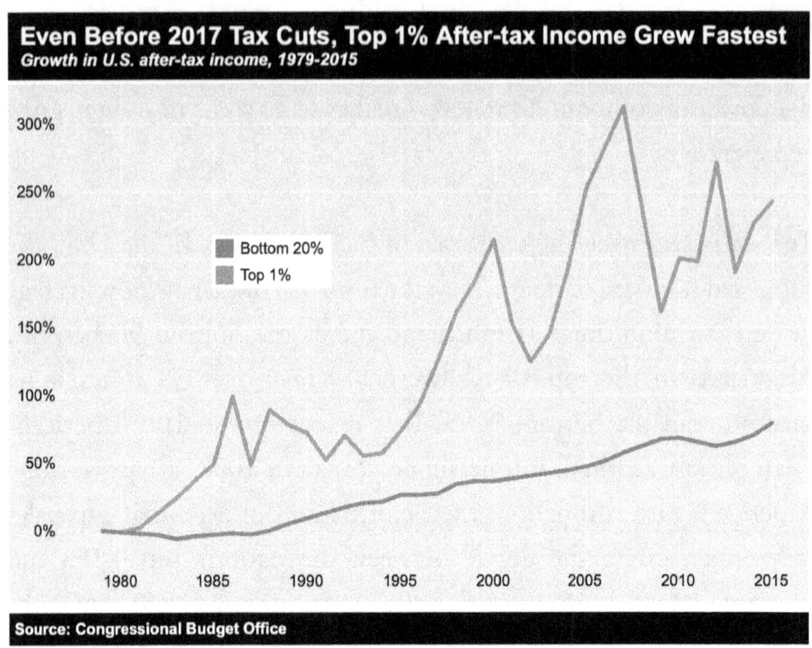

Figure 9: After-income tax comparison over time.

There are many legitimate reasons why some people earn so much more than others. Doctors earn more than janitors, for example, because their expertise, knowledge, and responsibilities are much greater. Differences between incomes are not necessarily the problem, but rather the fact that these inequalities are continuously growing is concerning. The nation's highest 0.01% and 0.1% of income-earners have seen their incomes rise much faster than the rest of the top 1% in recent decades. Both of these ultra-rich groups saw their incomes drop immediately after the financial crashes of 1929 and 2008, but they experienced a much swifter recovery after the more recent crisis. Income concentration today is as extreme as it was during the "Roaring Twenties." Since 1979, the before-tax incomes of the top

1% of America's households have increased more than seven times faster than those in the bottom 20. As a result, the top 1% used to control a little over 30% of the total wealth. They now control 40%.

The wealthy have many tools available to them that are not available to most others. Most poor and middle-class earners have to sell their time and labor, a finite resource, which limits their earning potential. The wealthy, however, can leverage their cash to grow it significantly, through the wonder of compound interest. Higher U.S. income groups earn a larger share of income from investment profits, which passively earn interest. This disparity has contributed significantly to increasing inequality because of the preferential tax treatment of long-term capital gains. Currently, the top marginal tax rate for the richest Americans is 37 percent, while the top rate for long-term capital gains stands at just 20 percent.

The most effective tool to make money is, ironically, money. So powerful is the effect of compound interest, which Albert Einstein once quipped was the 8th wonder of the world, that the wealthy could earn significant sums with little to no effort, by simply investing it in any number of funds and collecting the dividends.

These vast sums of wealth create wider-spread economic troubles when they are hoarded and not cycled through the economy. The top 1% often have more money than they can spend, resulting in cash laying idle in bank accounts and adding little economic value. This leads to wealth concentration, the process by which, under certain conditions, newly created wealth concentrates in possession of already-wealthy individuals or entities. Accordingly, those who already hold wealth have the means to invest in new sources of creating wealth or to otherwise leverage the accumulation of wealth. Thus, they are the beneficiaries of the new wealth. Over time, wealth concentration can significantly contribute to the persistence of inequality within society. Thomas Piketty, in his book Capital in the Twenty-First Century, argues that the fundamental force for divergence is the usually greater return of capital (r) than economic growth (g) and that larger fortunes generate higher returns. In other words, whilst the majority work for money, the wealthy are able to make money work for them.

There are numerous reasons why the past decade has seen further growth in this income inequality. Tax policies are a significant contributor. Logically, the less the wealthy are taxed, the greater the disparity. Progressive tax policies are the obvious counter to this, with higher earners having to pay greater proportions of their earnings in tax. Yet, governments are not keen on increasing tax rates for high earners out of fear of losing their support. This often goes hand-in-hand with another issue; rent-seeking. Rents rise when markets are not perfectly competitive, such as when uncompetitive markets yield monopoly profits or preferential regulation protects entities from competition. For example, a firm might be willing to sell a piece of software for $20 based on costs and a reasonable return to capital. But if the firm has no competition, it may be able to sell the same product for $50—the $30 difference reflects an economic rent.

The U.S. is, and has been for a long time, susceptible to lobbying and fixing rents against their organic prices should they have been left without interference in a competitive market. This had led many

Democrats and economists to argue that the U.S. economy is rigged. Joe Stiglitz, an American economist who was awarded the Nobel prize, describes how concentrating wealth in fewer hands means that it's easier for the wealthy in America to collaborate and get laws and regulations (such as anti-labor laws, free trade laws, limits to corporate liability, etc.) passed that make them even richer, creating a "feedback loop" that drives ever-greater levels of inequality.

Unfortunately, this brings with it higher levels of misery, desperation, sickness, and death for low earners, who comprise greater proportions of the population. The infamous Koch brothers are a prime example of this, where they used their wealth and power to suppress environmental concerns for decades in order to remove obstacles for their vast petroleum empire. This rent-seeking behavior shows no sign of regressing under conservative control. It has been noted that countries with a more left-leaning legislature generally have lower levels of inequality.

Advances in information technology has been identified as a key driver in this wealth divide. Erik Brynjolfsson of MIT has identified technology as "the main driver of the recent increases in inequality." In particular, information and communication technology (ICT) advances — such as in robotics, automated processes, machine learning, the Internet of Things (IoT), "big data," and artificial intelligence — are being blamed for making workers (primarily those with mid-level skills in medium-wage jobs) increasingly redundant.

Advances in technology and communications has fueled mass globalization and international trade. Globalization has been found to reduce global inequality between nations whilst paradoxically increasing inequality within them. When rich countries trade with developing countries, the low-skilled workers from rich countries may see reduced wages as a result of the competition, while low-skilled workers in developing countries may see increased wages through new demand opened by trading globally.

As income and wealth inequality becomes greater in magnitude, so too do the effects. The rising gap between the rich and everyone else has fueled unrest across much of the world, from Europe's ongoing Brexit crisis to the 2019 elections in India, where ordinary citizens have had enough of economies rigged in the wealthy's favor. A sharp reduction in extreme poverty globally has not diminished the sense of loss among middle-class and working-class citizens of countries with advanced economies. Stagnant wages for those who have had to endure a decade of austerity after the financial crisis of 2008 have really begun to stir resentment against those who continue to benefit at their expense.

This frustration can manifest itself in many ways. British researchers Richard G. Wilkinson and Kate Pickett have found higher rates of health and social problems (obesity, mental illness, homicides, teenage births, incarceration, child conflict, drug use), and lower rates of social goods (life expectancy by country, educational performance, trust among strangers, women's status, social mobility, even the quantity of patents issued) in countries and states with higher inequality. Numerous studies have also shown that social cohesion, economic growth, and political stability can all diminish as the inequality gap increases. Conversely, crime and debt have been found to increase.

It is not a new concept. Yet, income inequality has continuously increased over the past decade, showing no signs of abating, especially in the U.S. The divide is driven to new heights due to a combination of increasingly sophisticated technology, rent-seeking from influential groups of elites and the simple fact that economic disparity is a feature of free-market capitalism when the rate of return of capital is greater than the rate of growth of the economy. This, in combination with stagnant wages of the middle classes, has pushed the issue into the limelight and turned it into a heated political issue.

We can expect this issue to become a major talking point in the next U.S. presidential election, as many Democratic nominees use it against their conservative peers. Only diligent political policy can solve this issue in the near future through strategies like investments in education, which has proven a key tool in lowering income inequality. Access to high-quality education raises incomes and promotes growth by building human capital and the productive potential of the poor. In the meantime, the divide will continue to increase as the wealthy become wealthier at everyone else's expense.

Data

iSpy

Anonymity in the twenty-first century is now virtually impossible. Tech giants such as Apple, Google, and Microsoft track your phone's movements through location-based services, pinpointing your exact location wherever you are. Google scans your emails in order to barrage you with more targeted advertisements. Apple stores all your private iMessages, and Dropbox reads your saves files. In fact, through code snuck into your mobile phone, Google knows nearly every Wi-Fi password in the world. Even if it were somehow possible to lead a normal life without any attachments to technology, something virtually unimaginable nowadays, CCTV cameras and facial recognition technology can track your every movement the second you step out of your house. The saying, you can run, but you can't hide, has never been so apt.

The sheer scale of data harvested through all manner of methods and devices is unfathomable. Phones, voice assistants, and vehicles are constantly collecting data even when not in use. With the inevitable rise of the Internet of Things (IoT) and mass interconnectivity through superfast 5G networks, even mundane devices such as a toaster and washer will be seeking to extract any information it can find. All this data has become vastly valuable to marketers who are paying fortunes for information, which can more accurately help them target their customers. With great power comes great responsibility. Yet, companies and governments, the largest collectors of data, have proved unable to secure data from those who wish to use it for immoral means.

In 2020, data production is estimated to grow to 44 times the level it was in 2009, with experts estimating a 4,300% increase in annual data generation. Individuals are responsible for 70% of this data creation, with 80% of it stored by enterprises, of which over one-third is stored on the cloud. The value of this data has created great profit opportunities, both legitimately and illegally. According to

Statista, an online portal for statistics which reports on the number of data breaches and records exposed in the United States since 2005, the number of cyber-attacks is on an upward trend. In 2005, 157 data breaches were reported in the U.S. By 2014, this had quintupled to 783, with at least 85 million total records exposed. Just three years later, that number more than doubled into 1,579. Those who find themselves exposed to such breaches are often small and medium-sized companies who would rather pay the relatively small ransoms to get their operations back. Paying a $5,000 ransom, no matter how immoral, can avoid much larger costs when companies are shut down for weeks at a time. Figure 10 shows the growth in data breaches by sector.

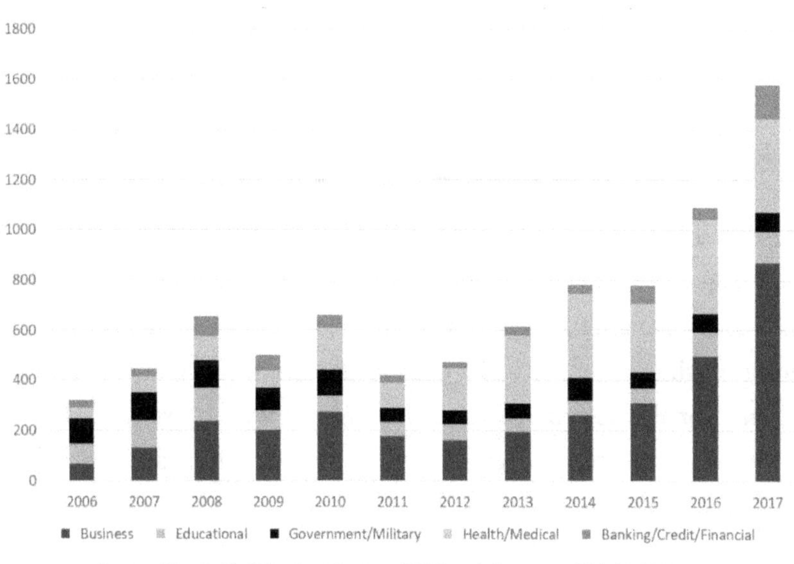

Figure 10: Data breaches by sector over 20 years.

There have also been many blue-chip data breaches in the past decade.

Marriott, eBay, Target, and Uber are some big names who have fallen victim to sophisticated cyberattacks. Wikileaks created great notoriety in the early part of the past decade when it published more than 90,000 internal U.S. military logs of the War in Afghanistan in 2010. The documents revealed numerous cover-ups and the absence of trials for captured or killed Taliban members by the coalition, much to the displeasure and embarrassment of the U.S. government. A further 392,000 U.S. Army field reports of the Iraq War, the largest leak in the history of the U.S. military was also disclosed a few months later, documenting multiple cases of misconduct, abuse of power against civilians and other war crimes by U.S. authorities in the country. The leaks also showed that Iran was involved in the war by supplying Shiite militias with deadly weapons.

In April 2016, 11.5 million confidential documents were leaked from the Panamanian law firm Mossack Fonseca which detailed the financial and attorney-client information of more than 214,488 offshore companies in an event now known as the 'Panama Papers.' The leaks revealed information of various prominent figures involved in hidden financial dealings within tax havens and companies doing business with terrorist organizations and governments under international sanctions. Shakira, the Duke of Westminster, Madonna, Bono, and even the Queen of England were all found to be hiding tens of millions away from tax authorities.

The most widespread data breach by far was by Yahoo in 2014 when it (eventually) reported that account details across a colossal 500 million users had been compromised. Sensitive information, including names, addresses, passwords, and telephone numbers, were all hacked. The once-dominant Internet giant, while in negotiations to sell itself to Verizon, announced it had been the victim of the biggest data breach in history, likely by "a state-sponsored actor." As if this wasn't bad enough, Yahoo then announced a couple of months later that it had buried the disclosure of another breach in 2013, by a different group of hackers that had compromised 1 billion accounts. Besides names, dates of birth, email addresses, and passwords that were not as well protected as those involved in 2014, security questions and answers were also compromised.

In October of 2017, Yahoo revised that estimate, saying that, in fact, all 3 billion user accounts had been compromised. The breaches knocked an estimated $350 million off Yahoo's sale price. Verizon eventually paid $4.48 billion for Yahoo's core Internet business. The agreement called for the two companies to share regulatory and legal liabilities from the breaches. Yahoo, founded in 1994, had once been valued at $100 billion. These breaches alone were enough to end the reign of this once giant. After the sale, the company changed its name to Altaba, Inc.

Although much smaller in scale than the Yahoo breaches, the now infamous Cambridge Analytica scandal of 2018 was perhaps the most disturbing of data breaches this past decade. Cambridge Analytica's controversial influences over recent major events such as Brexit and the U.S. presidential election in 2016 have brought to light the consequences of what happens when too much data is utilized without proper and thorough regulation. Cambridge Analytica had started collecting data on Facebook users since 2014 via a personality app. Cambridge Analytica used the 300,000 people who downloaded the app to pull further information from their friends via Facebook's' Graph API interface, through which third parties can interact with Facebook's' platform. An estimated 87 million users are thought to have had their personal data collected by Cambridge Analytica through Facebook alone. They also claimed on their own website that they held over 5000 data collection points on each of the 230 million Americans.

This provided enough information to build the psychological profiles of millions of people and target political messages to them to sway political opinion. It presented a great cause of concern in a nation which prides itself as being a flag-bearer for democracy and freedom. Cambridge Analytica claimed they always acted within the law. Even if true, there is a significant ethical concern when using bots to spread the news and fake stories. The company has since closed down due to both existing and new clients avoiding a company of such scandalous news, but have the company has covertly launched under the new company name of Emerdata. The damage has been irreparable.

Facebook CEO, Mark Zuckerberg, testified before Congress over the data breach and has admitted to his part in the lack of protection and control of its collected data to prevent political manipulation and has since vowed to tighten the platform user's control of data. More than $100 billion was knocked off Facebook's market capitalization in just a few days. This is the first real, meaningful pushback against such unethical data giants and has opened both the individual users' and the government's eyes to the power wielded by those with access to big data. Since then, governments have become more active in regulating these giants, with introductions of new legislation and regulatory bodies encouraging greater accountability.

Facebook suffered a subsequent attack in September 2018 when nearly 50 million user accounts were hacked. Unlike the Cambridge Analytica scandal, in which a third-party company erroneously accessed data that a then-legitimate quiz app had siphoned up, this vulnerability enabled attackers to directly take over user accounts, highlighting concerning weaknesses for a company with access to so much private and damaging information.

Fortunately, some strong efforts have been made in recent years to avoid future breaches of this magnitude. The European GDPR (General Data Protection Regulation) law replaced the old-fashioned, and no longer relevant, existing data protection laws created in the 1990s with a new and up to date set of procedures and standards designed to harmonize data protection laws across Europe and ensure greater protection and rights for individuals. Among some of the main features is the need for parental permission to purchase data on children under 16, easier access to an individual's collected and stored data (the current £10 Subject Access Request will now be free of charge) as well as predefined fines for breaking of any of these rules.

The previous UK's ICO (Information Commissioner's Office) previously wielded a maximum fine of up to £500,000. The new GDPR rules raises this to a maximum of €10 million or 2% of a firm's total revenue for lesser offenses, rising to €20 million or 4% of a firm's maximum revenue for more serious offenses. These significant fines are hoped to not only deter companies from unethical use of data but also to raise the priorities for businesses about their data security. Within mere hours of the introduction of the GDPR laws, complaints were launched about Google, Facebook, Instagram, and WhatsApp for forcing users to accept the terms and conditions outside of the law. Potential fines of more than $3million for each company are being debated. The U.S. has yet to create similar data laws to the extent the EU has, and as such, will continue to suffer from further lax security by American companies.

The internet, and hence data and security, are still in their infancy, and much progress and change are yet to come. It seems inevitable that massive data breaches and attacks will become larger in magnitude and more widespread as data mining devices continue to saturate people's lives. Until government regulations, such as the new GDPR laws, really start to crack down on sloppy companies, and governments are given authority to prevent these companies from trading in data, change will not come soon enough.

Data collection activities will proliferate, both in quantity and the nature of its sensitivity. Even advances to the pacemaker have made this medical device vulnerable, where human hearts become sensitive data generators, creating potentially fatal consequences were they to become susceptible to hackers. Properties and performance of autonomous vehicles, such as Tesla's range of electric cars, are already able to be modified remotely from Tesla HQ. These abilities, when placed in the wrong hands, could have horrifying consequences. Still, technological progress should not be slowed for it has the ability to do much good. The key to successful implementation, therefore, lies in building suitable safeguards to ensure this progress is made safely.

Jobs and Employment

Work Smarter, Not Harder

Emerging from the depths of the Great Recession, it was inevitable that this past decade would see a change in the employment landscape. Surprisingly, employment is at an all-time high, despite constant fear-mongering by economists and politicians alike about threats of mass automation and the ensuing elimination of jobs. The opposite couldn't be truer. Whilst some jobs have inevitably been automated (as it has done, especially during the Industrial Revolution), many more have been created. The question is how long this will hold true, and if, one day, AI and robotics will become so sophisticated that it starts to eliminate more jobs than it creates.

The past decade has been a mixed blessing for employees As of May 2019, the UK had an all-time low unemployment rate of just 3.8%. The U.S. performs marginally better at 3.7%. As a result of these tight employment markets, wages have finally started to increase in line with growth as employers have to offer more competitive salaries to draw further labor. Yet the nature of work is taking a greater toll on workers. The ubiquity of smartphones and laptops means an employee is never really disconnected from his or her job, even when away from the office. And even at work, we are pushing ourselves harder than ever: four out of five workers usually eat at the office, skipping a genuine lunch break. They also are more likely than ever to work from home and participate in the gig economy. Increasing rents and house prices in many large cities are pushing workers to settle in the suburbs, increasing commute times and reducing time spent socializing. The consequences of this are decreasing levels of happiness for many.

America is part of a small club of nations that do not have any laws mandating a maximum length of the workweek, and U.S. employers are taking full advantage. Today, 77% of Americans work more than 40 hours a week, with one estimate by Ohio University pegging the average American full-time workweek at 47 hours. That's a lot more than people from other countries. The average American employee puts in 260 more hours a year than the average British worker and a staggering 499 hours more than most French citizens, according to statistics from the International Labor Organization. For reference, there are only 120 hours in a five-day workweek. Despite their best efforts to remain a valuable part of the workforce, the increasing saturation of technology has many in fear for their jobs, even though history has proven that technology does not necessarily harm employment rates. In fact, past revolutions have witnessed the opposite.

The industrial revolution of 1760 - 1840 is often cited as the first major economic adjustment period resulting from the introduction of new technologies. This transformative era brought about new manufacturing processes, a transition from hand production to machines, the introduction of new chemical and iron production processes, the increasing use of steam power, and the rise of the factory system. Combined, these factors raised Britain's manufacturing prowess and made it a major technologically-advanced country. Despite similar fears to those of today, such as these steam-powered machines taking jobs of those which used to be performed by man, the overall impact on the majority of society and the economy was positive. Even to date, the U.S. experiences net job growth most years, as shown in Figure 11.

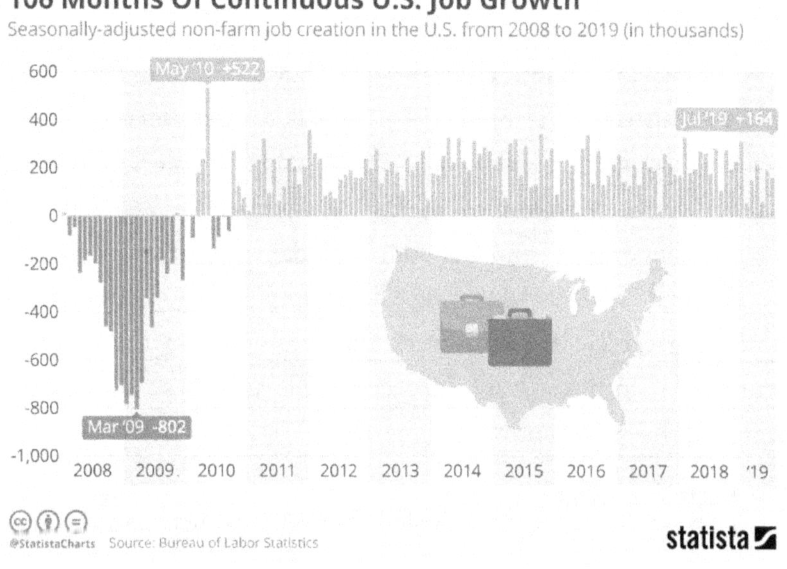

Figure 11: Net positive job growth over the past 10 years.

Introductions of technologies such as steam power and industrial machinery increased the productivity of individual employees and business as a whole, leading to increased wages and an increase in new jobs necessary to operate and tend to these new machines. Increased wages also had the secondary effect of stimulating consumer demand as people now had greater disposable income to spend on luxuries such as more nutritious food and leisure activities. This, in turn, upped the demand for new products and services, spurring business growth whilst also creating further jobs that foster the cycle of prosperity. Transport infrastructure also improved alongside the need to distribute these new products and people, further boosting trade. The larger distribution networks increased demand from businesses, opening new opportunities such as bigger textile mills that required more employees to cater to the new demand.

In retrospect, it is now clear that mechanization and automation of the industrial revolution did not lead to widespread suffering or major social upheaval as we fear of today's revolution. Instead, factory productivity improvements increased both wages and the total number of jobs, spurring consumer demand for more products and services, further increasing the supply for this demand and continuing the cycle. The growth that transpired in the following couple of centuries was unprecedented and has undoubtedly improved the quality of life today.

This has been the case with all revolutions to date. Industrial revolutions create more demand and, therefore, more supply, creating more new jobs than those which were initially lost. This past decade, however, has bucked the trend. We are now entering an unprecedented era where productivity, the main indication of increasing prosperity, is not rising despite the high employment levels. This has economists the world over scratching their heads yet again. Is there cause for concern, though?

Firstly, it is important to note the difficulty of accurately defining the root causes of the weak productivity experienced since 2000. There are many theories, some more positive than others. The statistical analysis techniques used to analyze productivity data have come under scrutiny as of late. Whereas manufacturing output from physical products, like manufacturing, is relatively easy to measure as it was during the industrial revolutions, measuring service sectors such as finance and the aerospace industry are much more difficult. Developed and richer countries tend to deviate away from manufacturing (as they outsource to less developed countries for cheaper costs) into service-based trading, which can return better profits thanks to the increasing ease of doing business globally. The UK, once a leader in manufacturing output, now has an 80% service sector-based economy, including sectors such as banking, insurance, and finance. Most developed countries follow this trend.

A second more bleak theory reckons that earlier waves of innovation in technology (computers, outsourcing functions, etc.) have fully saturated the economy and are no longer adding any further effect to it. This is further exacerbated by a lack of business investment as a result of austerity measures deriving from the financial crisis, as well as cheap loans raising the debt levels of companies in a period of increasing interest rates and high corporation tax.

But perhaps the biggest difference in this new era of automation is the nature of the jobs which are under threat. Whereas past revolutions have involved the automation of "mechanical muscle," this new wave of automation experienced this past decade involves "mechanical minds." Cognitive functions, such as creativity, problem-solving, and interpersonal skills, has long been man's greatest asset, separating us from other mammals in the animal kingdom. Yet, as AI becomes increasingly able to automate these inherent human capabilities, humans lose their leverage over the accuracy and speed of technology.

'Easy' jobs, therefore, will be the first to become automated, such as factory workers, office administrators, and data analysts.

These simple, repetitive tasks are easily replicable by technology. Perhaps further jobs will be created for those who design and build these new machines, however, resulting in a net positive gain. These new jobs, however, are far more intellectually demanding. Engineers and designers are the only tiers of workers able to create these new technologies. This will become a notable trend; as more blue-collar jobs are destroyed, the new wave of jobs opened by these new opportunities will be increasingly white-collar, demanding higher levels of qualifications and intellectual capabilities. Displaced blue-collar workers will not be able to fill this void without significant training, as many of them are mature, have family commitments, and do not have the resources to undergo training.

We are already witnessing an era of greater demand for engineers, designers, and IT staff, whose numbers are not increasing in line with the sheer amount of new jobs created in these areas. Their wages, therefore, are increasing whilst many of the lower classes of the workforce are suffering from decreased wages or complete redundancy. This will not be the case for all blue-collar workers; however, the need for on-call plumbers, for example, will always be present. But the general trend is unavoidable. Minimizing this effect will be down to the education policies of governments. Currently, not enough is being done to prepare future generations for these new emerging jobs or retraining those who are at risk to retool for new industries.

Many governments are, however, trying to prepare for an era of more disparate wages. Several schemes have been dreamt up, some more bizarre than others. Bill Gates has suggested a "robot tax" where robots which replace human workers are taxed at similar rates to what their corresponding human counterparts would have, in theory maintaining government income tax revenue streams. A negative income tax also has popular support among many economists, where a form of a progressive income tax system provides supplemental pay from the government to people who earn below a predetermined income level. While those above the threshold continue to pay tax to the state, those below will not be taxed but will see income given to them to meet the minimum income needed to live sustainably, hence the term negative income tax.

A more popular, and perhaps feasible, approach to limit the damages from potential automation, however, is a universal basic income (UBI). This would take the form of a new kind of welfare regime in which all citizens of a country receive a regular and unconditional sum of money for which a basic but livable income would be guaranteed. There would be no pressure or requirement to work, perhaps creating an understandable public outrage that it will create a lazy and unproductive society. The main reasoning behind this theory is to firstly ensure those displaced by robots do not fall into a state of poverty while also ensuring consumer spending does not drop to low enough levels whereby the economy would suffer. In its purest form, a UBI would be totally independent of income, meaning both the poorest and wealthiest would receive the same periodic income with no strings attached.

Several countries are either planning for or actively experimenting with different forms of UBI systems. Switzerland rejected such an idea in a 2016 basic income national referendum, with 77% of voters rejecting the proposal. Other countries have had more success. In 2017, Finland undertook a pilot program where 2000 citizens each received a monthly income of €560 ($640). Despite hopes for an extension after the initial two-year trial, the government has decided to halt the program to pursue other more promising opportunities. Kenya is also in the early stages of a smaller scale trial with results expected to be posted in the near future, while other countries such as Scotland are in the planning phases of the trial. The largest current trial is in Ontario, Canada, where 4000 participants have just been enrolled. The many trials which are either in progress or in the planning and enrolment phases have yet to show any results. Still, governments and economists everywhere will be eagerly awaiting the results of this ambitious theory.

Regardless of the outcome, there is no doubt that increasingly sophisticated technology and automation will have a substantial impact on the landscape of business and employment. History suggests that while "mechanical muscle" and now "mechanical minds" will fully or partially automate numerous jobs, the net effect on the economy will be positive as advanced technology brings about more jobs. There will be losers, especially those whose jobs revolve around repetitive and systematic jobs where computers are already infinitely better suited to. Yet there will also be winners for those who are able to enter these new markets. The bulk of newly created jobs are likely to be in these new nascent industries, often requiring qualified and intellectually capable labor for these new complex jobs.

How many are left behind in this new digital age will depend on how well governments can train and educate new potential employees, such as through education programs more tuned to a changing technological landscape. It also is subject to how well those who are at risk of redundancy can be retrained and retooled to fill new demands.

3. Science and Technology

Transport

Electric Cars

Changing up a Gear

In today's age of rapidly improving technology, tech-years can be compared to dog years. In just 10 years, electric motor technology has matured beyond all forecasts. Tesla, the current pioneer in electric motors, started the decade with revenue of $117 million, from sales of its then sole model, the expensive and somewhat gimmicky Tesla Roadster, which peaked at a mere 109 vehicles in the month of July. Today, with the introduction of the Model S in 2012, the Model X in 2015, the Model 3 in 2017, and Tesla's forthcoming Model Y (collectively spelled SE3Y through no coincidence) has not only transformed Tesla as a company but the concept of motoring as a whole.

In 2009, the global stock of PEVs (plug-in electric vehicles) was just 6000 vehicles. After the introduction of the Nissan Leaf and the Chevrolet Volt in late December 2010, the first mass-produced PEVs, plug-in sales grew to about 50,000 units in 2011, to 125,000 in 2012, and almost 213,000 cars and vans in 2013. Sales totaled over 315,000 units in 2014, up a whopping 48% from 2013. In just five years, global sales of light-duty plug-in vehicles increased more than ten-fold, totaling more than 565,000 units in 2015 - an 80% increase from 2014, driven mainly by increased demand from China and Europe. Continuing the trend, about 775,000 plug-in electric cars and vans were sold in 2016, and 1.22 million in 2017 - up 57% from 2016 - with China accounting for about half of global sales. The global market share of the new light-duty plug-in segment reached 1.3% in 2017, up from 0.86% in 2016, and 0.38% in 2014. Global PEV sales passed the 3 million mark in November 2017 and 5 million at the end of 2018. Figure 12 shows the growth of plug-in electric car ownership per capita in selected top selling countries.

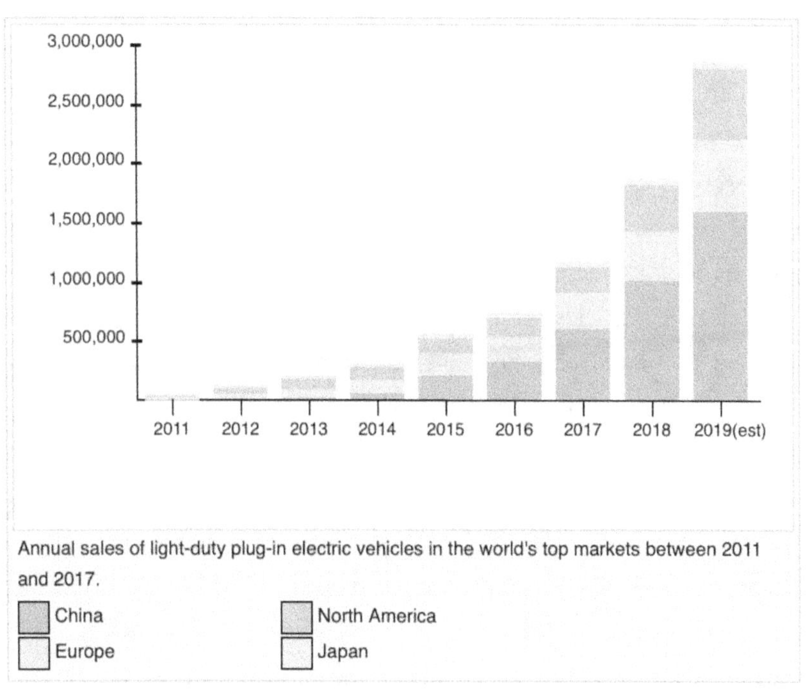

Figure 12: Growth of plug-in electric car ownership per capita in top selling countries.

Why is there such a rapid increase in electric vehicle demand? Perhaps the most dominant driver of growth is from government subsidies, where governments are keen to offer incentives to reduce demand on fossil fuels and hence CO2 and NOx emissions. Environmental sensitivity is starting to be of significance for many governments. The UK has emphasized plans for at least half of all new car sales, and up to 40% of new van sales, to be hybrid or electric as part of its 'Road to Zero' strategy. Perhaps rather ambitiously, it also plans by 2040 to end the sale of new petrol and diesel cars, and just 10 years later it wants almost every car on the road to be zero-emission.

Interestingly, Norway has the highest number of electric vehicles per capita in the world, as well as the world's largest plug-in segment market share of new car sales at 49.1% in 2018. As of 2018, 10% of all passenger cars on Norwegian roads were plug-ins. Doubling the benefit for the environment, most of Norway's electricity is drawn from a network of hydroelectric power plants, meaning most of these electric vehicles are consuming true renewable energy. Whilst Norway likes to emphasize that these figures reflect its desire to move away from fossil-fuel vehicles, it is important to consider the lucrative government subsidies and the fact that the average Norwegian is among the richest people in the world. This means that many of the country's citizens can actually afford a new electric car, the cost of which is prohibitive for many motorists outside of Norway. The fact that the country's wealth is largely derived from their vast sales of oils does not fit in with the image of eco-consciousness, however.

Environmental sensitivity, generous government subsidies, and electric vehicle's increased range and reduced costs have opened up electric vehicles to many of the middle class. This rapidly opening market has drawn players from all over the automotive industry, with many just starting to play catch-up due to the failure of foreseeing the spectacular rise of EVs (electric vehicles). Volvo and BMW have committed to going electric, inspired by Tesla's boom and a shift in consumer trends, by announcing that every car they produce from here on will be partially or fully electric. Mercedes is promising the same from 2020.

But while electric vehicles gather traction, supporting infrastructure is lacking. According to the 2017 English Housing Survey, a third of homes in the UK don't have off-street parking or places to charge their cars. With persistently low gas prices, many Americans see no financial reason to make the switch to an electric vehicle, especially as charging stations are few and far apart in most of the U.S.'s vast expanse of empty highways.

As both EV technology and the supporting infrastructure improve and costs are driven down, electric vehicles will become increasingly common. It is likely that eventually, petrol and diesel car sales will ultimately be completely phased out, but they will be not completely driven off the road anytime soon. Still, the International Energy Agency forecasts that the number of electric vehicles will grow to 125 million by 2030. As the crusade against crude oil continues to rage on, electric vehicles are currently emerging as the victor.

Self-Driving Vehicles

Power-Trip

Self-driving vehicles, otherwise known as driverless, automated, or autonomous vehicles (AVs), have been a staple of science fiction films for decades and usually denote a utopian era of innovation, minimalism, efficiency, and style. The film Minority Report (2002) showed densely packed autonomous pods ebbing in and out of traffic within inches of others at breakneck speeds whilst navigating multiple lanes and crisscrossing roads in such a seemingly complex series of maneuvers that it makes driving in Manhattan rush hour look like a Sunday stroll in the park. Total Recall (1990) featured Arnold Schwarzenegger riding in "Johnny Cabs"; autonomous taxis which somewhat resemble today's Uber – minus the simultaneously friendly and creepy humanoid drivers. Yet the past decade has seen great effort and progress made into the development of self-driving technologies, with great achievements. Every year that such advances are made, this dystopian future creeps eerily closer.

The basic premise behind AVs is that they are able to sense their environment and analyze data to make informed decisions. Doing this without crashing is even better. By using advanced sensing technologies such as radar, lidar, sonar, GPS, odometry and inertial measurement units, the artificial intelligence (AI) onboard these vehicles are able to take the "I" out of driving.

The Society of Automotive Engineers (SAE) has devised a numerical scale to represent differing levels of autonomy:

Level 0 - All controls are manually operated (steering, braking, throttle). This is what all cars up to 1960 have been and how the majority are driven even today.

Level 1 - Specific single functions can be automated such as the throttle via cruise control and steering via lane assist but not both at the same time, as this would be classed as level 2. Cruise control appeared on Cadillacs and Chryslers from around the 1960s. Although a specific function is automated, the vehicle is not, however, as a human must have control of the wheel or pedals at all times.

Level 2 - Specific functions such as those listed above can be combined to allow successful travel without a human touching the steering wheel or pedals. Cruise control and lane assist ensures vehicles travel autonomously without human interference, but a human must always be alert and prepared to take control at any moment. Whereas level 1 still requires human control, level 2 can be completely automated in some situations (motorway driving, for example).

Level 3 - Here, we shift it up a gear. In specific controlled environments, vehicles are completely autonomous and can take the driver to their destination without any input in operating controls from start to finish. Although there is no human input necessary, a driver must still be present and able to take control at any point during the journey. Currently, these vehicles are being tested by the likes of Waymo and Uber and are on the cusp of becoming commercialized. The use of level 3 vehicles, however, is limited to certain traffic and environmental conditions within which they are allowed to operate.

Level 4 - This is where a vehicle can finally be called truly autonomous. No human driver is required as the vehicle is safe enough to conduct all phases of the journey without interference. The key difference (and subsequent increase in difficulty) is that the human occupant need not pay attention to the road and is free to read a book, talk on the phone or even have a snooze. It is still bound, however, by certain driving limits and must operate within its "operational design domain" (ODD), where the environment in which they operate can be controlled. Waymo has chosen to jump directly into level 4 design, operating in specific parts of the city which are within the realms of control for the software.

Level 5 - Here, we finally have a fully autonomous vehicle in every sense and able to operate in all conditions. We are certainly a fair way off from this point, but this is the end goal, the point where autonomous vehicles become a utility. We simply enter our destination and think nothing more of it until we miraculously arrive. At this point, we are no longer driving, merely traveling as if one were on a bus or a train.

We are currently on the brink of Level 3. Audi's A8 is the first claimed Level 3 vehicle, using its "Audi AI" to transport its occupants autonomously up to 60kph in certain conditions that the software deems appropriate. There is a significant step between Level 3 and 4, however, the software required to make this jump will take years of data collection and continuous improvement to reliably and safely manage the unpredictability that comes with town driving.

Audi isn't the only company that has started investing heavily in autonomous vehicles. Waymo, a self-driving technology company, announced that it had begun testing driverless cars without a safety driver (an employee in the car had to be present at all times, however). In October 2018, it also announced that its test vehicles had traveled in automated mode for over 10 million miles, increasing by about 1 million miles every month. In December 2018, Waymo became the first company to commercialize a fully autonomous taxi service in the U.S. As of 2018, 29 states have now enacted some form of legislation related to autonomous vehicles. Even tech-companies from seemingly unrelated technology fields have jumped on the bandwagon. Apple's recently announced in May 2018, they also had a fleet of around 70 autonomous vehicles perusing the streets of the U.S.

Despite such large investments in this newly emerging field, a bumpy road lies ahead for this nascent industry. Many have legitimate safety concerns when it comes to entrusting the lives of their families and themselves to technology and artificial intelligence. In March 2018, there was a tragic death of a member of the public by an Uber self-driving vehicle in Tempe, Arizona, which made international headlines and dampened enthusiasm for the testing of such vehicles. The fact that this was the first death related to a self-driving vehicle despite millions of accident-free tested miles was not enough to control the onslaught of criticism aimed at this technology.

Until autonomous vehicles can prove that their safety far exceeds that of human capabilities, the uptake of AVs will waver, it is highly likely that this next decade will see towns and cities, especially those which are already heavily congested such as New York, London, and Paris, start to adopt physical zones where AV's are the only vehicles allowed. By utilizing fast 5G networks, self-driving vehicles can not only communicate which other vehicles but also infrastructures such as smart traffic signals and intersections.

Theoretically, this should allow for 100% safety statistics as human error, which is the root cause in almost 100% of accidents, would be eliminated entirely. Of course, these vehicles will be electric to avoid pollution concerns in delicate congested areas. They will also most likely not have a private owner but rather owned by ride-sharing and hailing companies like Lyft, Uber, Waymo, and Google, who are currently dominating the market. Introducing this technology to rural areas, where the environment is much more challenging to analyze and automate compared to urban areas, will take a considerable amount of time to automate if indeed it ever will.

No matter your thoughts, self-driving vehicles will become increasingly sophisticated and ubiquitous. Many areas stand to benefit from their introduction, particularly urban areas where road space and parking is sparse. But there are many obstacles to overcome before they are universally accepted. Many cite safety concerns, others simply enjoy the pleasure of driving.

Ride Hailing

All Aboard

The ride-hailing industry has exploded in popularity this past decade, with many companies, including seemingly unrelated tech giants such as Google, eyeing the rapidly expanding market. At the swipe of a finger, nearby private cabs can be instantaneously hailed at a very reasonable cost. At the end of 2019, the current hide-hailing champion Uber revealed it had almost 100 million monthly users after the company's founding just nine years prior. Having so rapidly changed the taxi industry, Uber was voted the second most disruptive company in the world, beaten only by Elon Musk's SpaceX. The statistics reveal why. Uber hosts 17 million trips a day (200 a second) and has made over 10 billion trips, covering 26 billion miles or the equivalent of 280 trips to the Sun. Available in 65 countries the Uber app is present on over 20% of all mobiles. Figure 13 shows the growth of ride-hailing trips vs traditional taxi services in NYC.

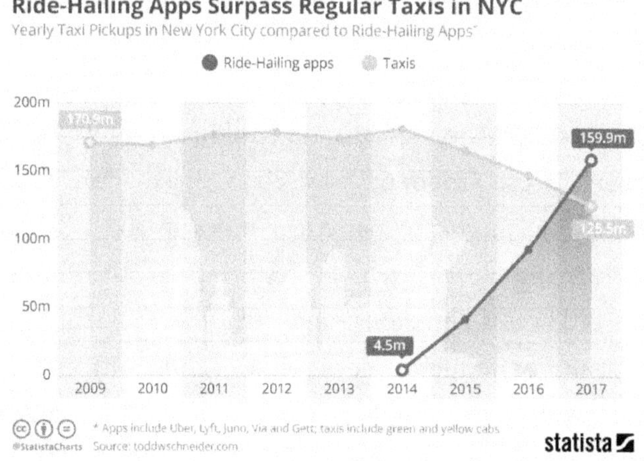

Figure 13: growth of ride-hailing trips vs traditional taxi services in NYC.

Surprisingly, cost is not the primary driver of such rapid growth of this industry, as is the case for most disruptive technologies, rather it is the convenience offered. The current cost for ride-hailing in the rich world is an average of $2.50 per mile compared to $1.20 for owning and operating a private vehicle. Despite ride-hailing currently costing over double the price per average mile travelled compared to conventionally owned vehicles, the convenience afforded by mobile-hailed vehicles is clearly a premium many are willing to pay.

It is perhaps of little surprise that almost all urban areas and city centers are of particular focus to ride-hailing companies. Privately owned vehicles spend, on average, 95% of their time unused, either sitting idly on the drive depreciating in value overnight or at work in the parking lot or parked on the street. Ride-hailing vehicles, however, can spend much more time in use, not only operating more efficiently but avoiding the wastage of limited space that parked vehicles occupy from already cramped city centers. Once autonomous, these vehicles can be kept active for almost 24 hours a day, barring charging and servicing times.

The benefits are clear to see. UBS, a banking firm, expects 80% of city travelers to use "robotaxis" by 2035. Even more boldly, they claim by 2030 a quarter of passenger miles in the U.S. will be in shared self-driving electric vehicles resulting in 60% fewer cars on city streets, 80% less emissions, and 90% less accidents. It is these last two points of reducing both vehicle emissions and accidents that entice governments to take advantage of and push autonomous vehicle legislation into the mainstream.

Still, it is the wallet that will most effectively convince commuters to drop the private car ownership model for good. UBS estimates that the driver comprises 60% of this average $2.50 cost per mile for ride-hailing. Automation will obviously eliminate this driver cost and, when combined with electrification and competition, predicts the cost per mile to drop to as little as $0.70 per mile. This presents significant savings, enough to surely tempt most drivers to cede control to machines. At this rate, a typical household driving an average of 10,000 miles annually could save $5,000 a year. This is music to the ears of the younger city dwellers whose main concern is being able to afford a place to live.

The explosion in vehicle miles travelled by ride-hailing companies this past decade was indicative of the general trend away from ownership models and towards a "sharing economy" from the likes of Airbnb to crowdfunding sites. Despite the unprecedented growth in vehicle miles travelled (VMT) from ride-sharing companies, the total still stands at just 1% of total VMT in the United States. We can only expect this to grow as city centers become busier, dirtier, and more expensive to live.

Technology

Artificial Intelligence (AI)

A Mind of its Own

Artificial intelligence (AI), love it, or loathe it, has subtly infiltrated both the home and workplace throughout this past decade. As hardware has significantly improved, so too has the underlying software which it powers. This rapid acceleration in software sophistication, from machine learning algorithms to deep learning neural networks, has allowed artificial intelligence to essentially program itself. It does so by coding the software to solve its own problems, and AI is now, to a certain degree, able to "learn" without the direct influence of human intervention. Scared? Perhaps we should be. But as much as there is to lose from ceding control to more intelligent sentients, there is much to lose in not utilizing it fully to improve mankind.

AI systems, which can perform certain tasks and problems far more efficiently than humans ever could, have the potential to solve some of the world's most logistically challenging problems, from accurately forecasting the effects of climate change to modeling life on other planets. Perhaps its superior intelligence might lead it to the conclusion that humans, with their inherently selfish instincts, are comparable to a parasite of the earth that rapidly consumes resources until the planet dies, compelling the AI to terminate the humans in order to logically yet disturbingly preserve the planet. Whatever the outcome, AI's continual improvement is a certainty, and our ability to utilize it to its fullest potential lies in first being able to control it.

We are certainly a long way off from any form of technological singularity, which is an event described as the point where AI becomes more intelligent than man, and thus the dominant "species" on the planet. Yet it is becoming ever more pervasive in everyday life. The past decade has seen the rise of AI-powered voice assistants such as Amazon's Alexa, Google's Assistant, and Apple's Siri, who have become increasingly more sophisticated and capable as they learn over time. At the end of 2018, there was a global total of 2.5 billion of these AI-voice assistants in operation. A 2018 Adobe Analytics survey found 32% of U.S. adults owned at least one smart speaker. The use of these speakers is still quite simplistic. However, 70% of surveyed owners used them most commonly for music, and 64% used them to check the weather.

Juniper Research, a digital market research specialist, expects the number of AI assistants to grow to 8 billion in 2023, more than the number of people on the planet. The majority of these voice assistants will reside on smartphones as these cheap devices spread to newly developing parts of the world. As more and more of these connected devices gather copious amounts of data about their users, they become ever more capable and much quicker. More promising uses of these smart assistants include complex actions such as shopping and food delivery, communicating with friends and family and performing actions around the house, such as switching on lights and activating alarms.

The voice assistant takeover is spreading to other devices too. Amazon has recently announced a range of Alexa-enabled devices in otherwise old-fashioned products like wall clocks and microwaves.

These are slated to include voice assistants and microphones. These products join a slew of others from third-party manufacturers, such as doorbells, security cameras, washing machines, fridges, appliances, robot vacuums, mirrors, and showerheads that have all been imbued with the likes of Alexa, Google Assistant, and other niche voice assistants born in recent months. Expect this saturation of voice assistants into household products to step up again this coming decade.

Mobile Computing

A New Tech Titan Takes the Throne

It's hard to believe the world wide web is just 30 years old. At the same time, it takes the average American to reach adulthood; the internet has transformed the world quicker than any other invention in history. Behind this explosion in progress lies the hardware that powers it; the personal computer. PCs allowed the average person to access an almost infinite amount of information in a matter of seconds, boosting productivity and economic activity by removing geographic limits that have restricted man since time immemorial.

It seems strange to consider, therefore, the demise of the PC. Yet this past decade has brought exactly that. Having sustained exponential growth in the 2000s, PC sales have been dropping annually as smartphones and tablets are now seeking to replace them. Reaching its height in early 2012 at nearly 100 million sales, PC sales have dropped to approximately 70 million at the end of 2019, and the trend is only expected to continue. Figure 14 shows the drop in PC sales over the past 10 years.

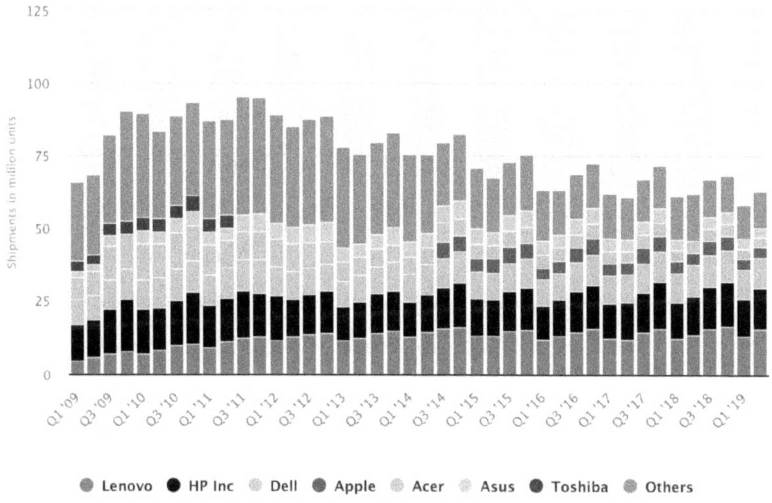

Figure 14: Decline in PC sales over the past 10 years.

You only need to look around or reach into your pocket to work out why. As PCs market share drops by 2.5% a year, tablet sales are increasing by around 9.6%, according to IDC, a network analyst company. Mobile web browsing has been steadily growing since 2009, while the desktop's share of web traffic has steadily decreased. In October 2016, the two crossed over, with global mobile and tablet browsing accounting for 51.3% versus the desktop's 48.7% - this is according to the latest data from web analytics firm StatCounter. It is easy to see why. Smartphones and tablets are portable and can be used anywhere, even in bed or chilling on the couch. PCs are typically limited to one per household due to cost and the likelihood of it being shared by the family. Smartphones and tablets are most certainly not communal devices, they are unique to the individual.

They are also a one-stop-shop; daily activities like shopping, banking, and communications are now done on a device no larger than the hand which controls it.

It is, therefore, no surprise that smartphones have reached near 80% saturation within most developed markets. The case is even more extreme in developing nations where the smartphone, now at rock bottom prices, provides the single point of internet access for these newly connected nations. They connect billions of people to the internet's plethora of information and services. Phones make markets more efficient, compensate for poor infrastructure in developing countries, and boost growth. Yes, they can be used for wasting time and spreading misinformation. But the benefits far outweigh the drawbacks. They might be the most effective tool of development in existence. After Nokia's crazy decline and ultimate exit from the mobile phone market in 2010, a whole host of competitors have risen to take advantage of this vast opportunity. From top sales of 231 million units in 2015, Apple singlehandedly dominated the smartphone industry with a 51% monopoly market share. Since then, Sony and Chinese tech company Huawei have far surpassed Apple's sales, but the industry still remains competitive, much to the benefit of the consumer.

It came as a surprise in 2018, however, when global sales of smartphones declined for the first time since a decade ago. According to the latest estimates from market research firm IDC, global smartphone shipments amounted to 375 million units in the fourth quarter of 2018, marking the fifth straight quarter of negative growth for the smartphone market. For the entirety of 2018, smartphone shipments declined by 4.1 percent to 1.4 billion units, making it the worst year ever in terms of shipment growth. High smartphone saturation levels in many regions and real innovations becoming rarer and less obvious to the average user, it was only a matter of time before the market reached this stage. The question is whether things will only go downhill from here. Or in other words, have we passed the golden age of the smartphone era?

Ryan Reith, vice president at IDC, cites longer replacement cycles, high penetration levels, and consumer frustration with rising prices as some of the factors contributing to the market's current weakness. With a new iPhone currently hovering around the $1000 mark, the lack of innovation and improvement, as seen in earlier days, is not persuading consumers to part with their cash, and they are holding onto older yet perfectly capable models. That weakness will likely carry on through 2019, as vendors continue to face challenging conditions, especially within China, the world's largest smartphone market. The imminent arrival of 5G devices does provide a glimmer of hope for the industry. Still, the more expensive hardware could drive up prices even further, potentially limiting the positive effect of 5G's arrival.

The start of the 2010s also marked the introduction of the now very iconic iPad. The hybrid phone-computer was a stroke of genius devised by the tech 'guru' Steve Jobs in his heyday. Like the smartphone, the tablet is a product no one knew they wanted but quickly became a staple of almost every home. Although tablets from a variety of electronics companies have cropped up all over the world, the iPad still remains the top player with a near 30% market share. Whereas competition has shrunk the iPhone's market share, no one has been able to match the simplicity, elegance, beauty, and performance of the iPad. By October 2010, a mere six months after its initial release, the iPad was selling like hotcakes, even beating the previously popular but now defunct champion, the DVD player, by a huge margin.

Tablets and smartphones will continue to dominate for the foreseeable future, it is only a matter of time before a new disruptive form of technology brings about its demise as it did to the PC. Wearable tech, such as smartwatches and optical devices, could one day provide a more convenient option to clasping around a large phone. With brain-computer interfaces now all the buzz in Silicon Valley, perhaps a day will come where computers will be fused with our organic brain, as Elon Musk's Neuralink Company is seeking to do.

Quantum Computing

The Future is Officially Here. Well Almost.

"If quantum mechanics hasn't profoundly shocked you, you haven't yet understood it." Such is the complexity of quantum mechanics that even one of the most intelligent scientists of all time was alleged to have said this. Physicists and computer engineers have been pondering quantum computing since the 1980s, where it has remained in the realm of science fiction for decades. This past decade, however, has seen some incredible milestones reached in the quest for a new form of computing power, with real and tangible uses on the cusp of development. If successful, quantum computing has the potential to open up areas of science previously thought impossible.

The need for a new form of computing is borne out of the fact that current transistors have become so advanced and so small that we are approaching the limit of what is physically possible. Thanks to Moore's Law, the empirical observation that the size of computer chips is minimized by half every 18 months, today's transistors have reached incomprehensibly tiny sizes of just 7 nanometers, which is 7 billionths of a meter. The physics behind nano-transistors has been found to simply break down, using quantum science, the science behind tiny particles, and presents unpredictable results. Quantum computing uses a radically new type of programming so unique to science; it has to be developed from the ground up.

There is no explanation necessary to understand the immaterial Importance computers have had on humanity and its progress. These conventional computers are built from billions of transistors that are turned either 'on' or 'off' to represent a value of either '1' or '0', in turn allowing classical computers to store and process data using 'binary digits' or 'bits.' In contrast, quantum computers process information using 'quantum bits' or 'qubits' that can be a 1 or a 0 or both at the same time (through the mystifying quantum effect known as superposition). A common metaphor used to compare the two is the simple flipping of a coin. In conventional computer processing, a transistor is either on or off, which could be compared to either heads or tails on a coin. But when asked whether that coin is heads or tails while it's spinning, the coin can be considered as both. This superposition, the ability to be in two states at the same time, is the fundamental concept in quantum computing. Instead of a conventional bit that's either 0 or 1, you have a quantum bit that simultaneously represents 0 and 1, until that qubit stops spinning and comes to a resting state. This allows for a far greater number of computations per second and, ultimately, much more computing power.

This past decade has witnessed a desperate race to build the first meaningful quantum computer. In 2016, scientists at MIT created the first five-atom quantum computer (referred to as a 5-qubit machine) with the potential to crack the security of traditional encryption schemes. Since then, the race has intensified. In 2018, Google announced its entrance into the market with its 72-qubit "Bristlecone" chip, which they claim is powerful enough to reach "quantum supremacy" (the point where quantum computing devices can solve problems that classical computers practically cannot). Not to be outdone. However, IBM, the trailblazer in quantum computing, unveiled their latest product in January 2019 with its initiative called IBM Q. Using this system, the IBM Q System One, the world's first commercially available quantum computer consisting of 121 qubits, was unveiled to the world.

In this rapidly transforming field, Google's latest Sycamore quantum computer appears to have performed, in just over three minutes, a task that, the researchers estimate, the world's most powerful classical supercomputer would take around 10,000 years to complete. This is a display of the niche (but not yet particularly useful) sheer power of quantum computing technology. Charging into the field as well as the incumbent transistor champion Intel, who is targeting production-level quantum computing within ten years and expects the technology to start to enter its "commercial phase" around 2025.

A common, and understandable question, many have regarding quantum computers is what can they be used for, and how will they revolutionize the industry? Perhaps the first meaningful use of the technology will be its ability to model complex molecular structures. This may sound like a specialist use for academics and chemists, but the results are far-reaching. Modeling the quantum effects on the nanoscopic level of molecules is not something which even the most powerful of supercomputers could ever do. But with the vast computing power afforded by quantum computers, these quantum effects could be modeled, allowing for a deeper understanding of chemistry, physics, and biology. This, in turn, would revolutionize our understanding of engineering and medicine and opening up new perspectives in areas such as cancer treatment and gene modification.

A direct future application of this could be to create a quantum simulation of your entire body and anatomy. Doctors (or AI) would then be able to run simulations of different drugs on your body. What takes months traditional trial and error on the use of drugs could be simulated in milliseconds with a quantum computer. This reduces that waiting time for human drug trials, which mostly fail before even reaching the market. The best available drug can be prescribed to you after just one consultation. Quantum computing may also hold the key to saving the climate from its current trajectory of permanent damage through running similar simulations. New materials can be invented along with new tools and construction methods for building. The possibilities are endless and can only be dreamed of with the use of conventional computers.

As with most nascent technologies, timelines are usually optimistic. The first transistor was introduced in 1947, and the first integrated circuit followed in 1958. Intel's first microprocessor, which had only about 2,500 transistors, didn't arrive until 1971. Each of those milestones was more than a decade apart. Many believe quantum computers are just around the corner, but history shows such advances take time. If 10 years from now we have a quantum computer that has a few thousand qubits, that would certainly change the world in the same way the first microprocessor did. Many are saying that quantum computers are between three and ten years away but it is likely that these people simply don't understand how complex the technology really is.

The hurdles ahead are incredibly complex and push beyond our current knowledge of physics. The chip, the backbone of any computer system, is just one little cog in a much larger system of gears. You also have to improve the enclosure to keep the delicate system running smoothly. Then there is the refrigeration needed to keep such masses of power cool; manipulating subatomic particles requires temperatures as close to absolute zero (-460 degrees F) as is possible. Qubits are extremely sensitive to pretty much any sort of influence. If the temperature were raised even a little bit, or the equipment knocked even in the slightest, the system would become critically unstable. Keeping the system free from errors and instabilities is extremely critical.

As the race towards the first commercially available quantum computers heats up, so too do the technical barriers. Yet it is a race worth running, as the benefits to humanity are mostly beyond comprehension with today's technology.

Internet of Things (IoT)

One Thing Leads to Another

On August 29th, as Hurricane Dorian hurtled towards the southeastern United States, entrepreneur and electric vehicle manufacturer Tesla's CEO, Elon Musk, announced that the owners of his trendy electric cars would find their vehicles had suddenly developed the ability to drive further on a single charge. Like an increasing number of modern vehicles, Tesla's products can be thought of as internet-connected computers on wheels. At the push of a button at Tesla's headquarters in Palo Alto, the firm was able to remove restrictions placed upon cheaper models to temporarily access full power of their batteries.

The internet of things (IoT) is a clumsy name for a big idea, but pretty self-explanatory one; it is the interconnectivity of internet-connected devices enabling information to be seamlessly shared between them. Legal scholars suggest thinking of the "thing" aspect as an inextricable synergistic mixture of hardware, software, data, and service. It may sound technical, but the internet of things essentially allows a plethora of devices to be remotely sensed or controlled through the internet to create a network of devices which can collect, share and act upon the information. By connecting devices such as washing machines, sinks, light bulbs, and kettles, the IoT becomes a sort of middleman between the previously untapped offline world and the online realm, allowing the collection of mass data from offline activities. This is touted to potentially help both consumers and producers create and use better products and services.

The Internet of things saw substantial growth during the 2010s due to advancements in wireless networking devices, mobile telephony, and cloud computing. Advancements in data processing, the growing utility of fiber-optic communication, and the rollout of 5G broadband allowed data and information to be dispersed among domains at faster speeds. Arm, a chip-design firm specializing in the type of chips the IoT needs, expects that by 2035, the world will have a trillion connected computers in circulation, hiding in all manner of mundane items from coffee machines to bridges and clothes. Figure 15 shows the explosive growth of this industry.

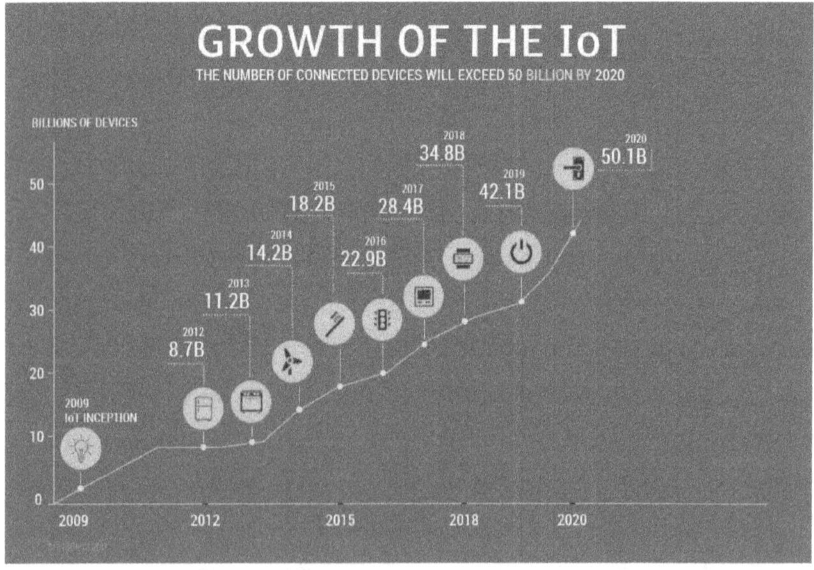

Figure 15: Growth in IoT connected devices.

The first wave of IoT connected devices over the past decade could be considered pretty basic. From fridges notifying you of dwindling milk supplies to coffee makers, which sync with your alarm to brew a fresh cup of Joe upon waking up, it appears that these inventions are hardly going to change the world drastically. With time and experience, more useful innovations such as smart thermostats enable households to become more efficient, reducing both the carbon footprint and the costs to consumers. Nest is currently one of the market leaders in this field and uses algorithms to learn of a household's routine, automatically adjusting the temperature needs of each individual home in the most efficient manner possible according to the occupier's personal circumstances. Savings to household bills from such systems save an average of 20%. When outside temperatures drop below freezing levels, the heating will automatically adjust to stop the pipes from freezing, and similarly, the algorithm will preset your air conditioning so you can arrive home to a perfectly acclimated home.

Although this may not seem revolutionary on an individual scale, the cumulative impacts, when applied globally to millions of households, would be incredible, significantly reducing the carbon footprint from buildings, saving users money, and significantly reducing and energy demands from power plants. Such gains are individually small, but when compounded repeatedly across an economy, the cumulative effects are potentially staggering.

It is not just the home where this technology has plentiful applications. High-tech buildings are becoming increasingly permeated with sensors and distributed computing that make up the IoT. GSMA

Intelligence, a research firm, forecasts that industrial uses of the IoT will overtake consumer ones by 2023, with smart corporate buildings leading the way. Many workplaces are now studded with hundreds of sensors which are integrated within the building's light fixtures, where they draw power and come with a low-resolution infrared camera, a Bluetooth networking beacon and sensors to measure many metrics such as energy consumption, air temperature and light levels. Individual sensors can collaborate with others to establish a wireless network working in synergy throughout the whole building.

Such sensors have all sorts of uses. They can keep track of daylight levels, ramping up the artificial lights on gloomy days, and cutting back on sunny ones. The result can be 30%-40% savings in energy consumption. Better lighting has also been found to boost employees' productivity by over 20%.

These technologies allow us to quantify things that used to be intangible. Sensors are even being applied to living beings in an attempt to extract data and improve efficiencies. Austrian firm Smaxtec has developed a sensor that can be swallowed. It lodges inside the reticulum, one of a cow's four stomachs. It stays there for the rest of the animal's life, monitoring body temperature, movement, and stomach acidity, and uploading the results whenever the cow is near a wireless detector. When fed to machine-learning algorithms, says Stefan Rosenkranz, who is Smaxtec's co-founder, this data can be used for many purposes. They can detect when animals are in heat and spot the early signs of calving up to 15 hours before it occurs. The sensor can also identify diseases several days before they become obvious to human observers, allowing early treatment and a 15-30%

drop in antibiotic use. A new sensor, due to be out next year, will add the ability to monitor digestion. Sales are doubling every year, says Mr. Rosenkranz. And with 278m dairy cows in the world, there is no shortage of customers.

Other uses are a little more concerning, however. In 2015 a pair of security researchers from Twitter and IOActive, a cyber-security firm, staged a demonstration for technology magazine Wired in which they remotely took control of a car that was being driven. They were able to turn on the stereo and the windscreen wipers, cut the engine, apply the brakes and even, in some circumstances, control the steering and braking. As a result, Fiat Chrysler, the car's manufacturer, announced it would recall 1.4 million vehicles. Security researchers have also demonstrated an ability to hack into medical devices, including pacemakers and insulin pumps. Even simple items, such as coffee machines, have come under threat. In June 2019, Avast Software, a Czech cyber-security firm, demonstrated how to install ransomware on a networked coffee machine, making it gush boiling water and constantly spin its grinder until the victim pays up.

As IoT is an unfinished technology, there will always be kinks to work out before the technology can mature. Despite the numerous setbacks and concerns, further growth in this promising field is a certainty, with new applications and new technologies creating many useful products and services. In the short term, some of the immediate beneficiaries will be industries like healthcare, agriculture and infrastructure where masses of data would enable clear identification of patterns and trends and therefore make accurate statistical predictions. Healthcare is one of the most exciting and promising industries which could be revolutionized into a new era of mass efficiency. Wearable tech such as smartwatches are already becoming hugely popular with an estimated one in six consumers who already own such items.

Market leaders such as Apple and Fitbit can track heart rates, movement, sleep, and calories burned, helping users makes informed decisions in improving regarding their health. On another level, internal body sensors such as pacemakers may allow for real-time monitoring of blood pressure, oxygen levels and blood cell count to automatically and immediately alert the relevant medical personnel of potential health issues such as strokes and heart attacks, the likes of which become significantly more damaging the longer they remain untreated.

Knowledge like this will allow medicine and healthcare to become more proactive as opposed to the current reactive healthcare model, offering significant benefits to all involved. Great Britain's NHS is already stretched thin financially in part due to an increase in life expectancy where over two-fifths of NHS spending is directed at those over 65 years old. Knowing the vitals of the elderly may enable paramedics to remotely diagnose problems such as low blood sugar levels or heart rates to potentially avoid expensive ambulance trips that might not be necessary.

On the macro level, IoT's potential uses become a little more disconcerting. We can expect cities to become "smarter" and edge closer to the "Big Brother" image of sci-fi cities monitoring their inhabitants. In Britain, councils are experimenting with infrastructure such as street lighting, which becomes extra bright when sensing shouting or hollering, such as in a mugging situation, thereby alerting nearby cameras to track those who are in the area.

Traffic lights with sensors are also becoming more common where computer algorithms track and monitor traffic flows in a bid to avoid cars sitting idle at traffic lights, which is responsible for 17% of the fuel burned in urban areas. Authoritarian China is already making use of such technologies. China monitors its citizens through the Internet and camera surveillance as well as through a social credit system and other digital technologies. Mass surveillance in China has significantly increased since Xi Jinping became the paramount leader in 2012. In 2019, Comparitech reported that 8 out of the 10 most monitored cities in the world are in China.

With a more in-depth and subtler integration of technology into society comes more profound suspicions and concerns regarding how much of our privacy can be held onto. The fact that so much information will be transferred without human input means the IoT could simply fade into the background and remain hidden from view. There are also concerns of an "always on" world where devices which require an internet connection to function will cease to operate without a live connection. This hyper-connected network poses problems for those who wish to go off the grid or live in rural areas. Also, pressingly, a digital divide may occur between those who have access to constant internet and those who do not.

There is also the concern of passing data privacy relating to the companies selling IoT devices and collecting its associated data.

The lack of clarity about where the data goes and who has access to it will also need to be addressed amid security concerns. One just needs to imagine a burglar hacking or obtaining a live feed from your security cameras to assess when the house is empty, to be concerned. As with most upcoming tech, these concerns are certainly valid, but with proper planning and further technological advances, they can be overcome. There is much to gain from a world of information connected in real-time. From automated cars to avoiding a heart attack, IoT will continue to infiltrate our lives. New upstarts will use the technology for purposes, perhaps unimaginable to us today. But public adoption will only grow so far if the associated security and privacy concerns are not addressed alongside them.

Medicine and Healthcare

CRISPR

Cut, Copy and Paste

Gene therapy, that is the transplantation of normal genes into cells with defective ones to correct genetic disorders, is heralded by the medical science world as a potential "miracle cure" for some of the world's deadliest and most feared conditions, such as cancer and cystic fibrosis. Genes have previously been thought of as permanent; genetic diseases are very difficult to treat, let alone cure. The past decade has lit the candle of hope that many of the most terrifying genetic diseases may not only be cured but potentially prevented.

The hope behind this new science comes from a new gene therapy technique called CRISPR (clustered regularly interspaced short palindromic repeats). CRISPR is not a medicine but rather a tool which can be manipulated to edit genomes - the complete set of genes or genetic material present in cells or organisms - by altering DNA sequences. The key to success lies in manipulating one particular protein called Cas9 (CRISPR-Cas9), an enzyme that acts like a pair of molecular scissors capable of cutting strands of DNA.

The science behind the Cas9 enzyme was actually first observed in nature after researchers studied the natural defense mechanisms of bacteria and archaea (single-celled microorganisms). These organisms, found commonly in nature, were observed using Cas9 enzymes to foil attacks by viruses and other foreign bodies by cutting and therefore destroying the DNA of foreign invaders. This is how the fundamental mechanism of the immune system works. Genetic researchers took an interest after realizing the potential of these natural mechanisms in the genetic manipulation of more complex organisms, such as humans.

Although the theory behind the science has been around for some time, no one really knew what the process physically looked like. It was only when a paper published in 2017 that it came to light. In the journal named Nature Communications, a team of researchers led by Mikihiro Shibata of Kanazawa University and Hiroshi Nishimasu of the University of Tokyo showed what CRISPR looked like in action for the very first time. Below is an image of the enzyme in action.

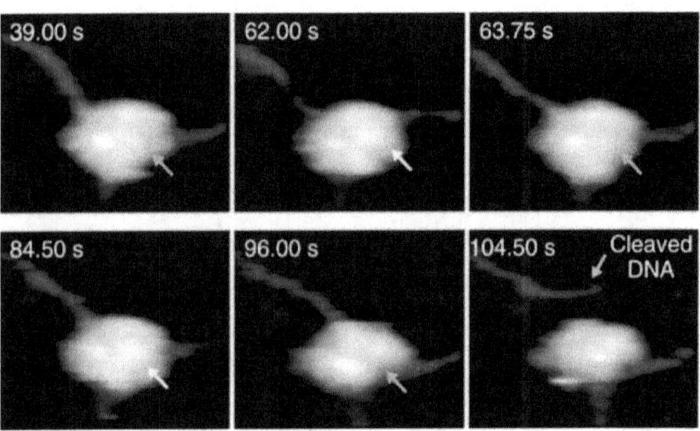

Figure 16: CRISPR gene-editing caught on camera.

Although these images may initially look rather underwhelming, what it represents is game-changing. The long darker brownish lines are DNA strands whilst the brighter yellow blob shows the CRISPR-Cas9 enzyme itself. The purple arrows point to the spot on the strand that CRISPR bites into, and the second piece of DNA, indicated by the white arrow, separates after CRISPR finishes clamping it off. The whole process, in all its magnificence, takes just 30 seconds. This video revealed, for the first time, a direct observation of CRISPR behaving just as researchers had long suspected it to.

It is still early days for this ground-breaking technology. It remains just a theoretical discovery, where the practical and tangible results could take years, perhaps decades away. Still, the research shows that gene editing is possible and full of potential. In theory, researchers can design their own RNA code to attach to any series of genetic code, such as a line of code suspected to be causing harm. This designed RNA code can then be mixed with the Cas9 enzyme and inserted into a living cell to either take the offending gene out of commission or repair the defective gene to allow it to perform its intended function properly. Although the few experiments that have been performed using this technology show some measurable success, the enzyme has been found to occasionally make cuts in the wrong place, thereby disturbing healthy genes.

Researchers have targeted their efforts on the HIV gene, too, showing much potential. In 2015 scientists managed to cut the HIV gene from laboratory samples, proving the concept. The following year saw the trial extended to live mice that were infected with the HIV virus in 99% of their cells. Injecting a CRISPR enzyme compound into the tails removed more than 50% of the infected cells from the test samples. Despite the success, there is still a steep hill to climb, but it is certainly worth exploring the viable premise that CRISPR or similar techniques could one day rid the world of HIV and other nasty genetic diseases.

Multiple companies are already utilizing CRISPR to diagnose genomes. Health company Human Longevity Inc. now offers an eight-hour physical exam called the Health Nucleus. Costing $25,000, it consists of an inside-and-out examination that includes whole-genome sequencing, high tech scanning, and early diagnostics. So far, the company has sequenced 40,000 genomes with demand rising and claims that one in 40 will discover they have an unknown serious cancer. As the cost and duration of these tests decrease, expect these sorts of examinations to become more common.

Other Medical Milestones

3D printing really came of age this past decade. Although most users of this technology to date have been basic and of small-scale use, mainly by universities and manufacturers, there is certainly a tremendous amount of potential once the technology and materials have matured enough. One example of a major milestone occurred in 2013 when researchers from Cornell University printed an outer ear that resembled and worked like the real thing. Researchers from the University of Pennsylvania and MIT have also reproduced blood vessels using similar 3D printing processes. Similarly, researchers at Wake Forest University in North Carolina were able to print skin cells onto wounds for rapid healing. A San Diego company called Organovo has also committed itself to printing human livers, and a 3D-printed partial liver transplant is expected by 2020.

Other exciting new medical applications for 3D printing include the printing of denture material such as crowns, orthodontic appliances, and dentures, as well as hearing aids and inexpensive customized prostheses for landmine amputees. There are many examples of successful prostheses that are, no doubt, providing a significantly improved quality of life for those affected.

Medical applications of 3D printing are also evolving rapidly, with 3D printed models being used to plan complex neurosurgical procedures, craniofacial reconstruction, and spinal surgery. The possibilities are truly endless once the technological barriers, including material sciences, have advanced enough. It could be very likely that one day, whether it be a new knee, skin graft, or even a new heart, a part of you will have been 3D printed.

The field of cancer has also seen some recent breakthroughs in its therapies. It is long known that cancer is one of the most debilitating of illnesses for both patients and their families. But new procedures such as including cancer "fingerprinting" give renewed hope. Cancer fingerprinting is a new approach to analyzing how specific cases of cancer react to different treatments. Every incidence of cancer has a unique fingerprint or identity code, and cancer fingerprinting allows medical staff to analyze the mutated genes of tumors and understand how sensitive various cancers will be to different types of chemotherapy.

Additionally, there have been advances in cancer immunotherapy, which treats cancer by boosting the body's immune system, rather than removing or targeting the tumor cells through surgery or chemotherapy. This has boosted life expectancies whilst minimizing the side effects of traditional chemotherapy treatments. Yet, the disease is still one of the world's top killers, with approximately 38.4% of men and women diagnosed with cancer at some point during their lifetimes. Until more efficient treatments surface, such as the potential of CRISPR for more targeted treatments, immunotherapy has offered some form of relief in this dark corner of the medical world.

The year 2013 also saw approval from the U.S. government to start the marketing of a bionic eye by California-based company Second Sight. The artificial eye uses a camera set into the user's glasses. This camera then transmits electrical messages wirelessly to the user's retinal implant. While it doesn't fully restore "normal" vision as you or I might sense it, it does enable certain patients to attain some level of vision with some patients having color vision restored.

Bionic eye development advanced further in 2016 in Australia when Bionic Vision Technologies was given $23.5 million in capital to develop their own version of a bionic eye. While it won't fully restore sight, it's hoped that it will restore enough vision to improve a blind person's level of function in their daily activities. The device is composed of a coiled antenna that sits on the back of the wearer's head and transmits information from a camera into the brain, bypassing the wearer's sightless eyes altogether. Trials started in 2018 and will take 6 to 12 months, with the results expected to be announced in 2019.

After a dry spell in results after its initial burst of enthusiasm in the

2000s, stem cell research produced some impressive achievements this past decade. In 2013, Japanese researchers succeeded in creating a functional human liver from stem cells. With this amazing breakthrough, the hopes of manufacturing artificial organs to save lives increased significantly. The induced PS cells (pluripotent stem) were grown into a working human liver in the body of a mouse. On 14 April 2013, the BBC carried out a report on a kidney grown in a laboratory in the U.S., which was successfully producing urine.

Many of the medical breakthroughs this past decade have been extremely promising. Yet their complexities make them incredibly difficult to bring into use. The next decade will most likely be of significant importance for research and early trialing, with results and commercial use not available until the end of the 2020s at the earliest. Yet the first step is always the hardest, and the theory at least is sound. It is only a matter of time before these medical technologies drive us into a new era of health.

4. Environment

Natural Disasters

When It Rains, It Pours

It seems barely a month goes by before another natural disaster is front-page news. Although nothing new, natural disasters such as storms, earthquakes, and floods are increasing in frequency and, on average, in intensity too. We have had some behemoth events before, such as the 1556 Shaanxi earthquake in China's Shaanxi province, which leveled 1000 square kilometers of terrain and killed an estimated 830,000 people who were buried by the ensuing avalanches. China seems to be home to the deadliest natural disasters throughout history, having lost an unfathomable 1-4 million people during the 1931 China floods and another 1-2 million in the 1887 Yellow River flood.

These gigantic death tolls are very unlikely nowadays; technology has allowed for effective weather warnings, and sophisticated infrastructure allows for effective evacuation and disaster management. Yet no amount of technology can currently change the intensity of these natural storms. In fact, there is much evidence to suggest that humans, in their increasing wisdom, capability, and knowledge, maybe indirectly worsening the frequency and intensity of these natural events. Never has this been more evident than in the past decade, and, thankfully, public awareness of the environment has gained significant traction.

The 2010s started with the worst natural disaster of the decade, and the death toll has placed it on a list of one the deadliest natural disasters in history. In 2010, just 12 days after the start of the new decade, Haiti witnessed a 7.0 magnitude earthquake which bought absolute carnage to Port-au-Prince. Haitian authorities believe that the disaster killed between 200,000 and 250,000 people, and over three million more were affected by the quake. About 1.5 million individuals were forced to live in makeshift internally displaced persons (IDP) camps. As a result, the country faced the greatest humanitarian need in its history. Weak political governance, lack of proper infrastructure, and limited access to basic resources means Haiti is still struggling to recover from this disaster. The relentless and continuing battle against natural disasters keeps Haiti vulnerable.

It wasn't just poorer countries that remained vulnerable. California in the United States battled ongoing droughts and water shortages for most of the decade. From October 1, 2011, through to 2016, California endured five years of record-breaking high temperatures combined with minimal rainfall, resulting in drought conditions unprecedented in at least 1,200 years, according to a journal published from the Geophysical Research Letters. On January 17, 2014, California State Governor Jerry Brown declared the drought a state of emergency. There is now considerable evidence that climate change was at least partly responsible for the dramatic reduction in precipitation during the winter rainy seasons of 2014 and 2015.

Researchers from Stanford University linked the unprecedented high-pressure weather patterns that blocked storms from California, known as the "ridiculously resilient ridge," to climate change. Others have also identified the effects of global warming in the emergent high-pressure patterns. Although rains have since ended this period of drought, the memories are still fresh, and concerns still remain. If future trends continue as they are and these episodes of natural drought continue, California and much of the dryer south-western states will need to seriously prepare for more of these damaging events.

Whilst California was dealing with limited water supplies, Texas had to deal with the exact opposite. The now infamous Hurricane Harvey in 2017 slammed into southeastern Texas after reorganizing over the Gulf of Mexico, causing catastrophic flooding and billions in damages. It became the first major hurricane to make landfall in the United States since Hurricane Wilma in 2005. Total damage from the hurricane was estimated at $198 billion, making it the costliest natural disaster ever in the United States. So intense was the aftermath of the hurricane, the World Meteorological Organization retired the name Harvey from its rotating name lists, due to the extensive damage and loss of life it caused along its track. This name will never again be used for another Atlantic hurricane and will be replaced with Harold for the 2023 season.

Having just recovered from nearly six years of drought, California then fell victim to unprecedented wildfires in 2018. Beginning in Northern California, the fires tore seamlessly through the once beautiful forests and hillsides, unable to be tamed by even the bravest of efforts by the California Department of Forestry and Fire Protection. It was not until nearly 2 million acres of California's forestry was burned that the fire abated, after which it officially became the deadliest wildfire in the United States since the Cloquet Fire in 1918 and the sixth-deadliest U.S. wildfire overall, killing 85 people and injuring 17.

If this wasn't enough to declare this decade the worst for natural disasters, the final nail in the coffin came from Brazil's Amazon rainforest, where savage wildfires tore through this globally significant piece of land. Wildfires blazed in multiple locations throughout the rainforest, and taming them seemed like a losing battle. Since January 2019, wildfires have propagated continuously and are thought to be caused by a slash-and-burn approach in creating new land for agriculture. Unusually longer dry seasons (the suspected result from environmental damage) and above-average temperatures worldwide during July and August are thought to have exacerbated the problem. As a result, 2019 alone saw 2.24 million acres of the rainforest burned.

Social Movements
All for One and One for All

The number and intensity of these natural disasters of the past decade have opened many previously closed eyes to climate change and its role in these disasters. Whether in poor Haiti or wealthy California, climate change is an issue that cannot be ignored or avoided. While still significantly under-appreciated, calls to action from ordinary civilians are becoming harder for governments and politicians to ignore, especially with the upcoming U.S. presidential elections in November 2020. This cannot come a minute too soon as current levels of environmental damage will soon approach irreversible levels. In order to keep a global temperature rise this century well below the 2 degrees Celsius above pre-industrial levels as per the Paris Agreement, the damage must not only be limited, but swift action must be taken to actively reverse already inflicted damage.

During the course of the decade, most of the world realized the severity of climate change, with more than half of the global population viewing it as a "very serious problem" in 2015 and giving broad support for limits on greenhouse gas emissions to address the issue. Concerns over plastic pollution grew considerably, with the effects of plastic waste on the Earth's environment gaining global awareness, particularly in the second half of the decade. New social media movement #TrashTag became popular when numerous Twitter users took to beaches, parks, and watercourses to clean up litter. In 2012, it was estimated that there were approximately 165 million tons of plastic pollution in the world's oceans. Plastic waste minimization initiatives were launched across the globe, with bans on various plastic products, ranging from plastic bags and straws to plastic cutlery.

In much of the developed world, charges of between 5-10 cents for disposable plastic bags are the new norm and have reduced Britain's plastic bag consumption by an impressive 86% since the introduction of a 5 pence charge in 2015. Plastic pollution appears to be highly linked to climate change with a 2019 report warning that by 2050, plastic could emit 56 billion tons of greenhouse gas emissions, as much as 14% of the Earth's remaining carbon budget. Whole swaths of products and industries arose, many centering on environmentally friendly products such as bleach and water containers.

The recent social movements surrounding climate change is of particular significance because it is extremely likely (greater than 95 percent probability) to be the result of human activity since the mid-20th century and is proceeding at a rate that is unprecedented across decades and even millennia. Technology has been the enabler of this movement, with Earth-orbiting satellites and other technological advances allowing scientists to see the big picture, collecting many different types of information about our planet and its climate on a global scale. This body of data, collected over many years, reveals the signals of a changing climate.

The Damage So Far...

The statistics behind our changing climate reveal the true extent of the current damage. Firstly, the climate is warming. The planet's average surface temperature has risen by about 1.62 degrees Fahrenheit (0.9 degrees Celsius) since the late 19th century, a change driven largely by increased carbon dioxide and other human-made emissions into the atmosphere.4 Most of the warming occurred in the past 35 years, with the five warmest years on record taking place since 2010. Not only was 2016 the warmest year on record, but eight of the 12 months that make up the year (from January through September, excluding June) were the warmest on record for those respective months. Ice cores drawn from Greenland, Antarctica, and tropical mountain glaciers showed the Earth's climate response to changing greenhouse-gas levels. Ancient evidence can also be found in tree rings, ocean sediments, coral reefs, and layers of sedimentary rocks, revealing that current warming is occurring roughly ten times faster than the average rate of ice-age recovery warming.

The true damage from a warmer climate lies in the melting of ice caps. Ice sheets in Greenland and the Antarctic have significantly decreased in mass. Data from NASA's Gravity Recovery and Climate Experiment show Greenland lost an average of 286 billion tons of ice per year between 1993 and 2016, while Antarctica lost about 127 billion tons per year during the same time period. The rate of Antarctica ice mass loss has tripled in the last decade. Melting ice results in greater volumes of water, with global sea levels rising about 8 inches in the last century. The rate in the last two decades, however, is nearly double that of the last century and is accelerating slightly every year. Compounding the problem is the fact that oceans have absorbed much of this increased heat, with the top 700 meters (about 2,300 feet) of ocean showing warming of more than 0.4 degrees Fahrenheit since 1969.

One of the hallmarks of climate change is that, on average, wet regions are getting wetter, and dry regions are getting drier. The Southwestern United States is one such dry region, and the Colorado River (which provides much of the water used in Southern California), is experiencing drought conditions unrivaled in nearly 1200 years. Yet in wetter climates, increasing temperatures results in greater atmospheric pressure, enabling it to hold and then release greater quantities of water, resulting in many of the flash floods, which have become more common. Threats to biodiversity are also becoming a greater concern. In its first report since 2005, the Intergovernmental Science-Policy Platform on Biodiversity and Ecosystem Services (IPBES) warned in May 2019 that biodiversity loss was "accelerating," with over a million species threatened with extinction. This particularly damages often poorer nations who are dependent on tourism for much of their income and who are in a weaker position to combat it.

Despite the masses of data, including research and evidence on the causes and damages of human-induced climate change, there is still a concerning number of opponents who think it is a hoax. This includes, rather embarrassingly, the current leader of the United States, Donald Trump. NASA's Climate 365 project has compared the predictions from four of the current leading environmental analysts, which all find similar trends in temperature increases over the past 150 years, as shown in Figure 17.

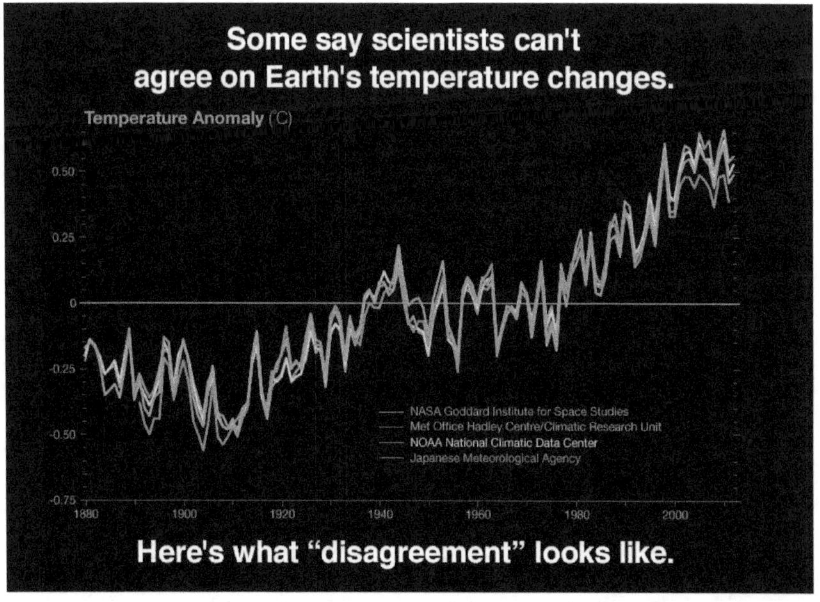

Figure 17: NASA's Climate 365 statistics for temperature change.

Much of the high-level denial surrounding climate change is not based on science but sadly on political agenda. The campaign to undermine public trust in climate science has been described as a "denial machine" organized by industrial, political, and ideological interest groups who are supported by conservative media and skeptical bloggers to manufacture uncertainty about global warming. Organized campaigning to undermine public trust in climate science is associated with conservative economic policies and backed by industrial interests that are opposed to the regulation of CO_2 emissions. Climate change denial has been associated with fossil fuel lobbyists, the Koch brothers, industry advocates, and conservative think tanks, most often in the United States. More than 90% of papers skeptical on climate change originate from right-wing think tanks. Although the demise of David Koch in August 2019 has released a large source of this denial, his infamous brother Charles and the myriad of other self-interested companies and lobbyists will ensure this organized denial continues whilst conservatives are still in power.

The Consequences...

The next decade will see all these trends above continue. On our current trajectory, temperatures will continue their slow but steady rise around the globe. India regularly experiences intense heat waves like in May to June of 2019, where the country witnessed one of the hottest and most prolonged heatwaves since records began, with temperatures reaching a scalding 123 degrees Fahrenheit. Greater heatwaves, both in quantity and intensity, can sadly be expected.

Extreme heat can overpower the human body and cause dehydration, heatstroke, and major organ damage. Certain demographics are more at risk from the impacts of heatwaves than others, including the elderly, children, and the poor. The Indian heatwave killed over 185 people in the state of Bihar alone.

Higher temperatures also prolong wildfire seasons in susceptible countries, as California experienced in 2018. Higher spring and summer temperatures and earlier spring snow-melt have resulted in forests that are hotter and drier for longer periods of time, creating prime conditions for wildfires to ignite and spread. Although higher temperatures are not a direct cause of wildfires (no matter how high the temperature a source of ignition is still required to start a fire), higher temperatures can create an environment where the chances of ignition are increased, as seen in the frequency of wildfires.

While higher temperatures reduce rainfall in dry states, they can also do the exact opposite in more tropical climates but still remain equally as dangerous. Higher temperatures increase the rate of evaporation of bodies of water and also augment air pressure. This, in turn, creates a surge in the amount of water clouds can hold, expanding the volume of precipitate and the intensity of its release, leading to intense rainfall and flash flooding. Very heavy precipitation events, defined as the heaviest one percent of storms, now drop 67% more precipitation in the Northeast U.S, 31% more in the Midwest, and 15% more in the Great Plains than they did 50 years ago.

Whilst weather and natural disasters are cyclical, more passive effects are borne from climate change. Since the beginning of the Industrial

Revolution, the acidity of surface ocean waters has increased by about 30 percent. This increase is the result of humans emitting more carbon dioxide into the atmosphere and hence, more being absorbed by the oceans. The amount of carbon dioxide absorbed by the upper layer of the oceans is escalating by about two billion tons per year. The atmosphere is also absorbing a lot of these pollutants, as in the case of dense cities such as Fahne in China pictured below in Figure 18. Both pictures were taken within just 10 days of each other.

Figure 18: Fahne, China regularly engulfed by smog.

The Future...

Heading into the near future, we can expect all these aforementioned trends to continue, with worsening consequences. The largest temperature increases are likely to be seen in the northern hemisphere across North American regions that usually have snow, such as the Rocky Mountains and northern Canada, as we have already experienced this past decade. These regions show such drastic warming because of the rapid melting and reductions in white snowcap areas. These areas usually reflect much of the sunlight, helping snowcapped areas self-regulate their temperature. Less white snow equates to more light being absorbed by the newly exposed darker rock areas underneath, which in turn reduces the critical reflective cooling effect. Less ice and snow mean more water. Likewise, the darker surface of the water absorbs further heat, in turn, warming water temperatures and further melting the remaining ice. It is this chain reaction of events which has climate specialists so worried about the future of our environment. At some point, it may become so bad it starts an exponential chain reaction of destruction that occurs too rapidly for us to stop or control.

Rise of Renewables

A New Lease of Life

Whilst we have lost many environmental battles, we have not yet lost the war. As much as our reliance on fossil fuels is contributing to a permanently changing environment, steps are at least being taken to wean ourselves off the black stuff. A beacon of light in this ocean of despair arises from the significant growth of renewable energy sources over recent years. From 2004, worldwide renewable energy capacity grew at rates of 10–60% annually for many technologies and this trend has continued throughout the past decade. According to the latest data from the Internal Energy Agency (IEA 2018), the world's total demand for energy grew by 2.1% in 2017, more than twice that of 2017. 40% of this growth was attributed to strong economic growth in China and India, of which 72% was met by coal, oil, and gas. Renewables contributed an impressive 25%, and the rest was provided by nuclear power.

This recent and unparalleled surge in the popularity of renewable energies is partly due to lower costs and increased efficiencies as the underlying technology and materials continuously improve. Despite recent setbacks in environmental policies, particularly America's withdrawal from the Paris Agreement (which aimed to limit global temperature rise to well below 2 degrees Celsius from pre-industrial times) an increasing number of governments around the world are waking up to the importance of addressing climate change quickly, whether it be the result of genuine concern or simply the recognition of shifting voter concern.

Brazil, for example, has one of the largest renewable energy programs in the world, involving the production of ethanol fuel from sugar cane. Ethanol now provides an impressive 18% of the country's automotive fuel. Ethanol fuel is also widely available in the United States, yet cheap gas prices and stubborn consumers ensure fossil fuels remain the primary source. Denmark is the current pioneer of wind energy, from which it now draws 42% of its total electricity consumption. Wind energy alone has, on occasion, produced a surplus of energy to the point where 100% of Denmark's electrical needs were met by wind energy for a short period of time.

Despite Trump's lack of action in combating climate change, not all states share his lack of concern. In 2015, Hawaii became the first state in the United States to formally commit to a plan of developing a 100% clean energy grid. California's state commission approved a plan in 2018 requiring solar panels for all residential buildings starting in 2020. Even China, who seemingly places the value of economic growth above almost all other socio-economic issues, began investing in clean energies to improve the air quality as air pollution reached critical levels.

Midway through the decade in 2015, global investment in renewables rose 5% to $285.9 billion, breaking the previous record of $278.5 billion in 2011. 2015 also marked the first year that renewables, excluding large hydropower, accounted for the majority of all new power capacities (134 GW, making up 53.6% of the total). This was a landmark achievement. Asia, the world's largest continent, is a substantial contributor to this rapid growth. Asia accounts for a sizable portion of the world's GDP, with the top five banks in the world being Chinese. In Southeast Asia, energy demands have increased by 60% in the past 15 years as rapid economic growth has spurred rapid industrialization. Figure 19 shows the growth of new investment in renewable technologies over a 13-year period. Although the trend shows a general increase in investment, peak investment occurred in 2016 and has declined since. Although many factors have caused this, predominantly less investment from China, it is highly likely that investment will eventually pick up again.

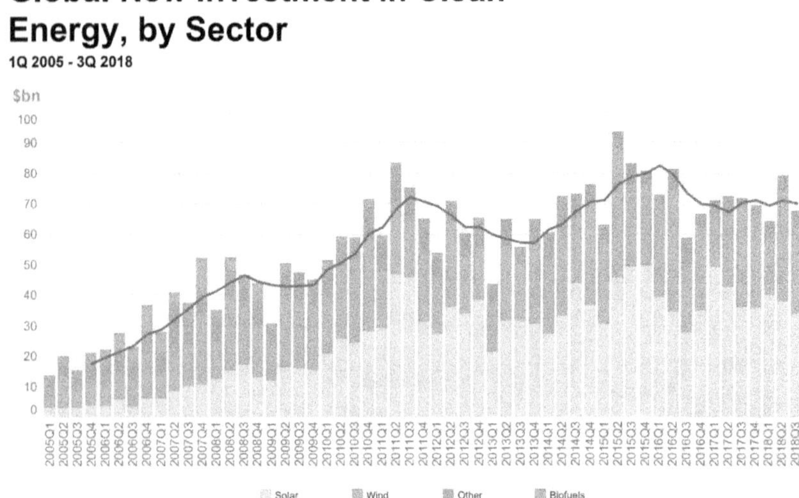

Figure 19: Global new investment in clean energy.

Despite the lowering cost of renewables and greater access to it, the sheer growth of developing Asian countries, especially China and India, cannot be sustained through renewables alone.

In such countries, where environmental legislature is weak at best and economic growth is the top priority of most governments, a lot of this growth is dependent on non-renewable coal, which is currently the cheapest and most accessible source of energy. Energy demands in India, despite being the third-largest contributor to greenhouse gases, after the U.S. and China, still remain comparatively small. Each person in India uses a 10th of energy that a U.S. citizen does. This is changing rapidly, however, with increasing prosperity and access to technology rapidly growing energy demands in developing countries. India's energy needs are therefore set to significantly increase as technology becomes more accessible, and income per capita increases. Only coal, the dirtiest and most inefficient energy sources, can currently meet this demand short term. As a result, BP has estimated that India's overall energy demands could double by 2040 due to further population growth and economic development, posing a significant concern for global carbon levels if this is to be met by coal.

With renewable energy sources now projected to account for more than a quarter of global electricity production by 2020, whole swaths of companies are now trying to leverage themselves into this hugely valuable industry. Although hydropower is currently the world's most widely-used renewable power source, with the global hydroelectric installed capacity exceeding 1,000GW, accounting for over 16% of the world's net electricity production and more than 65% of the global power generation capacity from renewable sources, the technology is fairly mature. It is wind and solar power where great technical strides can be realized, and profits can be made. The scalability of these two sources also greatly broadens their markets and use, making them potentially very lucrative businesses.

Wind energy is a particularly attractive form of energy generation because operational costs are essentially zero (wind is free). Once mass-produced, wind turbines can be made relatively cost-effective. Commercial turbines can be as tall as a 20-story building with blades over 200 feet long. The largest wind turbines currently in commercial use can generate enough electricity in a year to supply about 600 U.S. homes. Wind farms can have hundreds of these turbines lined up efficiently in particularly windy spots. As with most forms of renewable energy, the key to success lies in location, location, location. The debate rages on as to whether onshore or offshore farms are the best solution.

Onshore wind farms are relatively inexpensive, proving just slightly more expensive than coal per MW (not accounting environmental impacts, however, where coal costs considerably more). Offshore farms such as those far out in the ocean can harvest much more wind energy that can, on average, be 90% stronger than those on land. Offshore farms have much larger installation and operational costs – roughly double – and are much more complicated to integrate into a grid. However, they do alleviate aesthetic concerns that land-based turbines attract. Either way, we can expect to see more wind farms arise, especially along with coastal and mountainous areas where winds are generally stronger and more consistent.

Solar power will certainly continue to gather steam and will likely become the dominant source of renewable power in the near future. In 2015, worldwide-installed photovoltaics capacity increased to

227 gigawatts (GW), which was sufficient to supply 1% of global electricity demands. Just two years later, in 2017, this grew to 385 GW. Two forms of solar power currently show huge promise and are relatively mature: photovoltaics (solar panels) and CSP (concentrated solar power). As of 2014, an estimated 90% of installed solar power in the U.S. consisted of photovoltaic installations that are currently widely adopted the solar scene.

In a similar manner to how computer chips double in computing power every couple of years, research and development into photovoltaics has experienced similar rapid progress. Few industries have seen their growth accelerate in the way the PV industry has, with incentives such as America's Million Solar Roofs program and the inclusion of renewables within China's five-year plan for energy production creating an environment where solar panels are commercially viable, opening the technology to competition and exposed to innovation and price reductions.

Solar power is forecasted to become the world's largest source of electricity by 2050, with solar photovoltaics (solar panels) and concentrated solar power (large mirrors which reflect light into a superheated concentrated point) contributing 16% and 11%, respectively. Like wind energy, however, solar power is hugely dependent on geography. In the right environment, it can be very efficient. Data obtained from the MIT Energy Initiative showed, as expected, that solar power is at its highest during the middle of the day during the summer months. When the sun is 60° above the horizon, the sun's intensity is around 87% of its maximum (when shining on a horizontal surface). Drop this angle down to 15%, however, and the intensity quickly drops to just 25%. Looking more seasonally, a light cloud cover will produce a solar output of approximately 80%, whereas a heavy overcast day will drop that to a mere 15%.

This is not such a large problem for highly insulated locations (areas exposed to the sun's rays) such as California but has a profound effect on the viability of solar power in other areas. Even in the UK, which is seen as moderately suitable for solar power, a solar panel will produce 10 times less energy in December than in June. This drops to 65 times less when comparing a sunny day in June to an overcast day in December.

Aside from solar power being beneficial in suitable geographical areas, it is in developing countries where the biggest benefits reside. Investments in renewable energy were higher in developing countries than in developed ones, with China leading global investment at a record US$126.6 billion. In rural and remote areas, it is not the creation of power plants themselves that are the most expensive part of connecting people to the grid; rather, it is the transmission and distribution networks that remains logistically challenging and often prohibitive. Producing renewable energy locally can offer a viable alternative to these issues, and developing countries are seeing more of these mini-grids installed, especially in more isolated areas.

Take Nigeria, for example. Nearly 60% of the country's 190 million inhabitants lack access to reliable electricity, according to the government's Nigeria Power Baseline Report, with 75% of rural dwellers being cut out. Despite being one of the world's largest producers of oil and gas, and the largest producer of hydropower in West Africa, a variety of issues has plagued the country's power-producing capabilities. Droughts have stalled hydroelectric plants, and rebel attacks on critical gas pipelines in the volatile south have crippled power plants (gas generates 85% of Nigeria's electricity). In 2016, Nigerian militants destroyed vital gas pipelines in a bid to pressure the government to help the poor and clean up environmental pollution in the resource-rich but neglected region. Nigeria's current power plants can generate about 13,000 megawatts of electricity; they are not used at full capacity and produce only 4,000 megawatts because of gas shortages, an inefficient grid network, poor maintenance, and technical problems.

To combat these issues in a timely and efficient fashion, it has turned to solar mini-grids to increase electricity access and bolster energy security in Africa's most populous country. Six pilot solar mini-grids operating since early 2018 in five Nigerian states provided 15,000 people with access to reliable electricity. The mini-grids were partly funded with 1.7 million euros from the European Union and the German government in collaboration with Nigeria's state governments. The Nigerian energy companies Rubitec, GoSolar, GVE, and Nayo Tropical Technologies planned, built, and run these mini-grids.

By 2020, Nigeria wants to have plans laid for more solar mini-grids that would eventually reach more than 100,000 people. Solar mini-grids are not a new concept worldwide, but they are an increasingly popular way to provide low-cost, reliable electricity to rural areas. In Nigeria, they have the potential to give 26 million residents access to electricity, according to GIZ, the German aid agency that supports the initiative.

The scarcity of electricity will only deepen as rapidly growing countries demand more energy. According to the United Nations, Nigeria's population is projected to double to 400 million by 2050 and could reach one billion by the end of the century. Mini-grids are a feasible way to ensure this expanding population has a reliable source of electricity, which is a key contributor to growing prosperity.

Man's involvement in increasing CO2 levels and the resulting environmental damage have been major issues for decades. The 2010s marked the first decade where the need for positive change and action became universally accepted as a necessity. Despite Trump's continual denial, the importance of preventing (and eventually reversing) a warming climate is emerging as a prominent priority for governments and businesses in developed and developing countries alike.

Renewable energies such as wind and solar power offer some of the cleanest energy generation possible. However, the intermittency of both the sun and wind makes it unreliable for the majority of countries without significantly overbuilding these systems to compensate. In the meantime, the burning of coal is the current largest threat to the climate, especially in rapidly expanding countries such as India. Nuclear power is the most logical short-term substitute, offering some of the most efficient, available, and safest forms of power than other alternatives.

5. Society and Culture

LGBT and Gender Movements

Times Change

"It was very traumatic," recalls Arif Jafar, 47, outside the Indian Supreme Court, where a landmark ruling was delivered. "Being denied drinking water ... being beaten up every day just because of my sexual orientation was a really horrible experience. It took me almost 17 years to even talk about it," he said. Unfortunately, stories such as Mr. Jafar's are still a common occurrence across much of the developing world. Throughout the past decade, much of the western world has made significant progress in this movement of social acceptance for the LGBTQ+ world.

A record 4.5% of American adults now identify as LGBT, according to a new Gallup estimate. The percentage, which works out to more than 11 million U.S. adults, is up from 4.1% in 2016 and 3.5% in 2012. The report identifies the increase as being driven primarily by millennials, defined as those born between 1980 and 1999. In 2012, 5.8% of this millennial cohort answered "yes" when asked, «Do you, personally, identify as lesbian, gay, bisexual or transgender?" In the 2017 estimate, this jumped by 40% to 8.2% of millennials. In contrast, the LGBT-identification rate of older generations was found to be steady.

Whilst there may not necessarily be more gay people than in previous times, the greater numbers largely boil down to increasing social acceptance of the LGBT population over the last decade, which encourages more people to open up about their orientations. These changes have also been more pronounced in younger populations. Today›s youth have peers and social networks that are more supportive of LGBT people and similar issues when compared to older generations. Millennials have also been found to be significantly more accepting of LGBT rights than their older counterparts. According to a 2017 NBC News poll, 75% of those surveyed aged between 18 and 34 supported same-sex unions, compared to just 42% of those over 65. This is quite a staggering, yet unsurprising disparity.

The Netherlands "came out" first by becoming the first country to allow same-sex marriage in 2001. A plethora of countries have since followed suit. As of July 2019, 27 countries followed the Netherlands ‹ lead in validating same-sex marriages. This number looks set to rise. The United Nations Human Rights Council passed the UN›s first-ever motion in June 2011, condemning discrimination against gays, lesbians, and bisexuals and commissioned a report on the issue. Soon after, Barrack Obama became the first U.S. president to express his support for gay marriage. In May 2019, Taiwan became the first Asian country to legalize same-sex marriage, and Botswana made some progress by decriminalizing homosexuality in June 2019. This is especially significant for an African country where 34 of the continent's 54 countries still outlaw homosexuality. Kenya›s Supreme Court, for example, upheld laws that criminalize gay sex. By 2019, more than 70 countries continued to criminalize gay sex, most of them Muslim-majority countries or former British colonies, according to advocacy groups.

Whilst progress was accruing in much of the world, LGBT rights supporters continued to face legal obstacles elsewhere, with laws curbing the expression of homosexuality introduced in Russia and China. The United States was late to the party considering its claim as the "Land of the Free," having only legalized gay marriage in 2015 after the Supreme Court ruled that refusing to grant marriage licenses to gay and lesbian couples violates the Fourteenth Amendment to the United States Constitution. The U.S. has had some recent setbacks, such as the Trump administration›s attempt to reinstate the ban on transgender people serving in the military and the rescission of protections for transgender students. Still, social acceptance of gay people in America is resiliently at an all-time high among both democrats and republicans.

The transgender movement, of which many of its proponents feel dissonance over their personal identity and birth sex, also moved into the public arena this past decade, having gained significant publicity after celebrity Caitlyn Jenner (formerly Olympic gold medalist William Bruce Jenner) came out as a transgender woman in a 2015 interview. Jenner came out as a Trans woman, saying that she had dealt with gender dysphoria since her youth and that, «for all intents and purposes, I am a woman.»

Research from the Williams Institute suggests that there are at least 700,000 other transgender people in the United States, representing a small but still significant 0.3% of the total population and about 3.5% of the LGBTQ community. Nevertheless, these estimates are likely conservative because of the limited amount of studies that have attempted to measure the transgender population. Similarly, in the

EU, 1.5 million people classified as transgender, also representing 0.3% of the population.

Though some people seek to change the gender of that which was given at birth, the notion of even having a gender also came under question. Gender neutrality is the idea that policies, language, and other social institutions (social structures, gender roles, or gender identity) should avoid distinguishing roles according to people›s sex or gender, in order to avoid discrimination arising from the draconian prescribed social roles for which one gender is more suited than another. Gender movements such as feminism rightly aim to place the status of both men and women at the same level. A new group of people who identify as "non-binary" (a spectrum of gender identities that are not exclusively masculine or feminine) aims to eliminate any reference to gender altogether. This can involve discouragement of the use of gender-specific job titles, such as policeman, fireman, and stewardess in favor of equal gender-neutral terms such as a police officer, firefighter, and flight attendant.

An ongoing social and political battle now rages hard between those who deem gender a binary scientific notion of male and female based scientifically on chromosomes and those who wish to be identified as something else based on their internal beliefs and values. Many non-binary people who wish to identify as something other than male or female demand the use of new gender-neutral pronouns, such as 'they.' The list of pronouns which people self-identify as exists now in the dozens, such as ze/zir, hir, hirs, hirself and xe, xem, xyr, xyrs, xemself. In 2012 a gender-neutral pronoun «hen» was proposed in Sweden, and in 2014 it was announced that this word would be included in the following edition of the Swedish Academy Glossary. Sweden thus became the first language to have a gender-neutral pronoun added by an authoritative institution. «Hen» should now be used to describe anyone regardless of their sex or gender identification.

Whilst it is undoubtedly an excellent mark of social progress that people who identify as LGBT can now marry, adopt children and generally be comfortable with themselves, it seems as if the seesaw of social acceptance has tilted too far in the opposite direction, causing fiery debate among those on the left and right of the social spectrum. While everyone is free to identify themselves as whatever they wish, be it a he, hir, sie, or even a giraffe, demanding others to do the same seems to infringe upon the free speech rights of those who only identify as male or female as science dictates. To be forced to address people with these new gender-neutral pronouns can be seen as equally disrespectful to those who do not believe in it. The line between fact and feelings is a difficult one to clearly draw, but hopefully, time will set the appropriate boundaries for both sides of the debate.

Greater acceptance of the LGBT society requires the slow but steady pace of community consent, which is different from past times. This is the same for the acceptance of all races, creeds, and religions, which has made much of the Western world a more civilized and productive place. It is only a matter of time before sex and gender discrimination becomes a thing of the past. Hopefully, Mr. Jafar will one day be able to enjoy his old age knowing his children and grandchildren will never have to suffer as he once did.

Sexual Misconduct

#MeThree

"He told me he liked Chinese girls. He liked them because they were discreet because they knew how to keep a secret. Hours later, he attempted to rape me". The "He" in this victim's abhorrent statement could have referenced any number of sexual predators this past decade. The number of accusations of sexual assault by the wealthy and powerful have been seemingly endless, with consecutive news stories rapidly unravelling the sheer scale of this endemic. The case above refers to the now infamous and outcast Harvey Weinstein, a former American film producer who is currently awaiting trial for over 80 claims of sexual assault.

Weinstein catalyzed other victims to speak up and name their assaulters. Among the accused are many notable and once highly respected figures such as Michael Jackson, R. Kelly, Kevin Spacey and Morgan Freeman (most deny any wrongdoing). The movement also infiltrated the American political scene, with influential names such as conservative D.C. judge Brett Kavanaugh and 10 members of the United States House of Representatives. "I just start kissing them, it's like a magnet. Just kiss. I don't even wait. And when you're a star, they let you do it. You can do anything. Grab them by the pussy". These harrowing words were recorded in 2005 of U.S. President Donald Trump.

The scale of these harassment claims is truly astonishing, and the details utterly disturbing. That people in a position of the wealth of power have been able to get away with such crimes is profoundly depressing, yet perhaps not particularly surprising. Money and contacts seem to go a long way in protecting the accused. Thanks to the power of social media in providing a forum to bring to light many of these disturbing cases, however, it is becoming increasingly harder for these sorts of crimes to remain hidden.

Accusations of sexual misconduct are nothing new, and the intensity of accusations greatly increased as a result of the momentum created by the #MeToo movement. What started as a movement against sexual harassment and sexual assault following sexual-abuse allegations against Harvey Weinstein, it soon began to spread virally in October 2017 as a hashtag on social media in an attempt to demonstrate the widespread prevalence of sexual assault and harassment, especially in the workplace. Having first been tweeted by actress Alyssa Milano at noon on October 15th, 2017, the #MeToo tweet had been used over 200,000 times by the end of the day, and over 500,000 by the end of the next.

On Facebook, the term was used by more than 4.7 million people over 12 million posts during the first 24 hours alone. Facebook also reported that 45% of users in the United States had a friend who had posted the term, highlighting the breadth and depth of this misconduct. Once the ball started rolling, however, the momentum kept on unravelling scores of new victims. Tens of thousands of people, including hundreds of celebrities, replied with their own #MeToo stories, including male actors such as Terry Crews and James Van Der Beek, highlighting that women were not the only victims.

Film and media were not the only industry which was plagued with misconduct. In November 2017, the variation #ChurchToo was started by Emily Joy and Hannah Paasch on Twitter in an attempt to highlight and stop the sexual abuse that happens at church. In January 2018, a live-streamed video admission by Pastor Andy Savage to his church revealed that he had sexually assaulted a 17-year-old girl twenty years prior when acting as a youth pastor whilst driving her home. Savage finally resigned from his staff position at Highpoint Church just weeks after, but furiously only after having received applause from his church congregation for admitting to the incident and asking for forgiveness, revealing how many religious circles turn a blind eye.

The common denominator linking these waves of allegations is the nature of those accused. They are people of great power who abuse their positions using wealth and influence and intimidate their victims into silence while manipulating the justice system. Nowhere was this better highlighted than by the Presidents Club scandal, a male-only, London black-tie charity event, attended by 360 figures from various business, political, and financial scenes, held every year at the Dorchester Hotel. The 2018 event revealed the extent of how little regard this wealthy elite has for sexual harassment, demeaning the hostesses of the event who were instructed to wear "sexy black shoes" and black underwear and fell victim to groping and lewd propositions. A whole host of financiers, politicians, and celebrities were present, including Dragon's Den star Peter Jones and founder of hedge fund Duet Group, Henry Gabay. The elusive club has since shut down amongst universal outrage, a progressive step for such a secretive club.

Entering 2019, one would have hoped that the worst of the decade was finally behind us. The world saw justice prevail after the eventual arrest of rapper R. Kelly in July 2019. Kelly was accused of many heinous crimes including marrying then 15-year-old singer, Aaliyah (whom he had entered into a relationship with three years prior), 10 alleged counts of sexual abuse against four women, three of whom were minors at the time of the incidents. There was also the accusation by a former partner who claimed that Kelly "intentionally" infected her with a sexually transmitted disease.

All sense of progress was lost, however, after the unearthing of a vast network of underage sex trafficking by one of the U.S.'s most wealthy, powerful, and secretive businessmen, Jeffrey Epstein. First charged in 2008 with soliciting prostitution from underage girls, Epstein only served a short jail sentence thanks to a plea deal widely seen as far too lenient, indubitably due to his vast network of connections and wealth.

Epstein's crimes included installing concealed cameras in numerous places on his various remote properties to allegedly record sexual activity with underage girls by prominent people for criminal purposes, such as blackmail. Ghislaine Maxwell, Epstein's close companion, told a friend that Epstein's private island in the Virgin Islands was completely wired for video, and the friend believed that Maxwell and Epstein were videotaping everyone on the island as an insurance policy. It was also reported that Epstein's mansion in New York was wired extensively with a video surveillance system. Epstein allegedly "lent" girls to powerful people to ingratiate himself with them and also for gaining possible blackmail information to further his hold on his elite network of contacts. According to the Department of Justice, he kept compact discs locked in his safe in his New York mansion with handwritten labels that included the description: "young [name] + [name]." Epstein partially confirmed that he had blackmail material when he told a New York Times reporter in 2018, off the record, that he had dirt on powerful people, including information about their sexual proclivities and recreational drug use.

Among some of these "close friends" whom he often invited to his private resorts are two famous presidents; Bill Clinton and Donald Trump, two high profile figures who have both had their fair share of previous accusations. Eerily, Trump said of Epstein back in 2002: "Much of Epstein's "social life" involved very young women. I've known Jeff for fifteen years…Terrific guy. He's a lot of fun to be with. It is even said that he likes beautiful women as much as I do, and many of them are on the younger side."

According to Joseph Recarey, the lead Palm Beach detective on the case, Epstein was essentially operating a "sexual pyramid scheme," incentivizing his victims to go out and recruit more underage girls for cash rewards. Brown identified about 80 women who say they were molested or otherwise sexually abused by Epstein, and some accounts suggest the total number may be much higher. Despite his years of paying his way out of trouble, whether through his vast wealth and contacts or through the use of his amassed library of blackmail, Epstein was arrested at a New Jersey airport upon his return from a trip to France. He was charged with sex trafficking and sex trafficking conspiracy in a federal court in New York. If convicted, he could have faced up to 45 years in prison, along with the forfeiture of his Manhattan townhouse, according to the New York Times.

Just as it appeared that one the world's most prolific pedophiles was about to finally be brought to justice, Epstein was found dead in his Manhattan jail cell on August 10th, where he was awaiting trial. New York City's medical examiner ruled his death a suicide. Yet, the suspicious circumstances around his death created a whirlwind of conspiracy theories, with President Trump himself suggesting there may have been foul play. Earlier that fateful week, two prison guards were suspended, and a warden temporarily reassigned from the ward amid widespread reports that 30-minute checks, required within Epstein's unit, were not carried out properly as the guards had apparently fallen asleep on the night of Epstein's death. This death represented the first successful suicide in 21 years at the maximum-security prison.

With such vast reported collections of blackmail among many of the wealthiest and high-profile elites worldwide, there is certainly no end of potential people who would have liked to have silenced Epstein. Although justice on this past decade's most heinous pervert was denied after the death of Epstein, there is still hope that the true depth of this atrocity will be revealed to all, including many of those who were involved in this sex trafficking scandal. Whether this truth can be brought to light even if it seems to be under the protection of many powerful individuals, who are trying to cover it up, remains to be seen. At the very least, some of these people will be subject to some sleepless nights.

Shifting Demographics

Nature or Nurture?

The end of the past decade has seen a significant shift in societal demographics. In 2019, millennials (those aged 23 to 38) will outnumber Baby Boomers (55 to 73) for the first time, according to Census Bureau projections, making millennials the largest adult generation in the U.S. now. In their young adulthood, millennials are, on average, more educated, more ethnically and racially diverse, and slower to marry than previous generations at the same age. Having come of age during the Great Recession, their economic picture is mixed. Even though young adult households are earning more than most older Americans did at the same age, they have less wealth. High house prices and greater student debts account for a significant portion of this wealth gap, and stagnant wages make it difficult to break from this slump.

While the 73 million Millennials have become the largest living adult generation in the U.S.u, the succeeding one, Generation Z, is now entering adulthood. Also known as the post-millennials or iGen's, Gen Z'ers (those born after 1996) are on track to become the most diverse and best-educated generation yet. Nearly half of Gen Z'ers are racial or ethnic minorities. They also follow the more liberal social and political opinions on key issues compared to those of all previous generations.

The demographics of young American families are also shifting. A growing share of parents are remaining unmarried or marrying later.

The number of U.S. marriage ceremonies peaked in the early 1980s at 2.5 million marriages. Since then, however, the total number of people getting married has fallen steadily to around 2 million marriages a year, half a million less despite a population growth of over 100 million. As a result, barely more than half of adults in the U.S. say they're living with a spouse, the lowest share on record, and down from 70 percent in 1967.

Of the parents living with a child, the share that are unmarried jumped significantly from 7% in 1968 to 25% in 2017. Part of this increase is due to a growing trend of unmarried parents cohabiting, as 35% of unmarried parents were in 2017. Over the same period, the share of U.S. children living with an unmarried parent more than doubled, from 13% in 1968 to 32% in 2017. The reasons for this decline in marriage rates are not certain. However, it may stem simply from generational changes. Sex outside marriage and cohabiting are now the new normal, compared with earlier times where it may once have been a source of shame. Inflated house prices are much of a bigger concern for the western world, which has made saving for a down payment more of a priority than splashing out on a wedding. With greater rights for both children and cohabitants, the need to marry for financial security is not as prominent as it once was.

Despite years of stagnant wage growth following the Great Recession, incomes are now finally rising in the U.S. with a household income at its highest level in 50 years. But this increase is not distributed equally. As income inequality between the richest and poorest continues to grow, it has been more pronounced among certain racial and ethnic groups. For example, the gap between Asians at the top and bottom of the income ladder nearly doubled between 1970 and 2016. Over that period, Asians went from being one of the groups with the lowest income inequality to the highest.

Rising incomes have not transpired into greater financial prospects, however. Real, disposable income for the middle class has not grown since the middle of the 2000s, despite incomes for the top 10% reaching new highs, the OECD calculates. The rising costs of education, health care, and housing and ever-increasing college fees are squeezing the middle classes both in the U.S. and abroad. Homes are more expensive relative to incomes, meaning many young adults are unable to start investing in one of the most common wealth-building tools. About 70% of baby boomers were already middle-class in their 20s, says the OECD, whilst that figure today is around 60% for millennials and trending downward.

The immigrant demographic has also changed, with the immigrant share of the U.S. population approaching a record high. According to a Pew Research Center analysis of the American Community Survey, 44 million foreign-born people were living in the U.S. in 2017, accounting for 13.6% of the population. This represents the highest share since 1910 when immigrants constituted 14.7% of the total population, but still less than the record share in 1890 when immigrants represented 14.8% of the total. According to United Nations' data, 25 nations and territories have higher shares of immigrants than the U.S., including some Persian Gulf nations with high shares of temporary labor migrants, as well as Australia (29%), New Zealand (23%) and Canada (21%). Recent political events such as Brexit, the election of Donald Trump and a combination of political rhetoric and a decrease in living standards for the average American, has pushed the topic of immigration into a negative light among conservative media outlets and voters. Despite this, most countries with high levels of migrants report a general consensus that immigrants strengthen their countries rather than burden them, according to a 2018 Pew Research Center survey of 18 countries that host half of the world's migrants. Immigrants were viewed positively in 10 of those nations, including the U.S., Germany, the United Kingdom, France, Canada, and Australia. Majorities in five countries, however, viewed immigrants as a burden: Hungary, Greece, South Africa, Russia, and Israel.

A relatively new demographic phenomenon has occurred recently. For most of human history, populations were young, and lives were short, yet around the world, populations are now aging, with some countries facing a severe imbalance between an old and dependent class and a younger, more productive one. This mass aging is primarily caused by two demographic trends. Most obviously, people today are living longer than before. Advances in medicine and a generally healthier way of life are facilitating longer and healthier lives. A second and less obvious cause of population aging is a decline in the birth rate. With lower birth rates caused by young families having fewer children and having them later in life, the average age of the population is rising with a smaller pool of younger people to draw upon. Immigration on great scales can also affect demographic aging, although this effect remains small.

Adding to this aging shift, the 2010s was the decade in which most baby boomers in developed nations retired, putting further pressure on pensions and other safety net programs. The consequences of an aging society were felt hardest in Europe and Japan, which were the first to experience substantial population decline. Over 20% of Japan's population is over the age of 65, making it the most elderly nation in the world and putting significant pressure on Japan's finances as an elderly population becomes more expensive to maintain as they grow older. This problem is exacerbated by a declining fertility rate and decreasing tax revenues as fewer people provide taxable income.

In the United States, proposals for revising Medicare and Social Security have become hot political topics, and strategies include raising the retirement age or adjusting benefit amounts. France has tried on a few occasions to raise the retirement age, but widespread demonstrations in opposition has thwarted much-needed pension reforms. Similar stories emerge in other countries with burdensome pension spending, including Greece, Spain, Germany, and the UK.

Today, current levels of aging populations are straining public purses, and future levels could lead to catastrophic financial damage for some countries. According to data from World Population Prospects: the 2019 Revision, one in six people in the world will be over age 65 by 2050, which is up from one in 11 in 2019. Also, in 2050, one in four persons living in Europe and Northern America could be aged 65 or over. In 2018, for the first time in history, people aged 65 or above outnumbered children under five years of age globally. The number of persons aged 80 years or over is projected to triple, from 143 million in 2019 to 426 million in 2050. At these record-high levels, significant welfare reforms need to be made, including the potential radical programs such as universal basic income and raising of the retirement age to offset lower tax revenues from a smaller tax earning group.

Youth Culture

Kids These Days

From the U.S. rockabilly scene of the fifties to England's swinging sixties, each decade seems to bring with it another era of nostalgia. The seventies gave us bell-bottomed trousers, and the rise of disco whilst the eighties introduced a wave of now-legendary films including Back to the Future, E.T., and Ghostbusters. Youth culture of the 2010s, however, seems harder to pin down. Although it is always hard to identify trends as they are unravelling without the advantage of hindsight, so categorizing the youth of the 2010's is not as apparent as one might think. One might even say they were a bit boring.

Every generation of teens is shaped by their social, political, and economic environments. Today's teenagers are no different and they're the first generation whose lives are saturated by mobile technology and social media. Technology in the past decade has become so sophisticated that a young person's whole world, from communication and school work to socializing and gaming can all be contained in the now-ubiquitous smartphone. Widespread internet use has been around for younger people's entire lives, and perhaps social media can be pinpointed as one of the biggest focuses for youth culture of the 2010s. Worldwide, 26.3% of the online population uses Facebook, with the average user having an average of 338 friends.

The iGens in particular - those born between 1995 and 2012 have never known an era without smartphones, with many creating Instagram accounts before even starting school. Surprisingly even young people recognize this as a problem, with a Pew Research Center report finding that more than half of teens say they spend too much time on their smartphones and 41% overdoing it on social media. The average teen was found to spend 23 hours a week on smartphones and other gadgets each week and apparently also checking their phone on average every 12 minutes. Their adult peers are not much better, spending on average 3.5 hours a day on mobile devices.

As wonderful as access to this technology can be, by allowing for more communication with friends and family, for example, or being able to track their health and fitness better, over-reliance has been found to cause issues. Experts worry that social media and constant communication have become so integral to teenage life that it promotes anxiety and can lower self-esteem. A survey conducted by the Royal Society for Public Health asked numerous 14 to 24-year-olds in the UK how social media platforms impacts their health and wellbeing.

The survey results found that Snapchat, Facebook, Twitter, and Instagram all led to increased feelings of depression, anxiety, poor body image, and loneliness. This is not surprising; many "Instagram influencers' and online personas post set up snaps of their best moments, which young teenagers tend to compare to their less extreme yet perfectly healthy and ordinary lives. Social media stars posting filtered and photoshopped pictures of their figures and fashion leave others feeling uneasy with themselves, creating a pandemic of body image issues.

Social media allows for constant communication with friends beyond the classroom, but the restless instant messaging means you can never truly escape it. A grave concern stemming from kids communicating more indirectly is that it has gotten easier to be cruel. "Kids text all sorts of things that you would never in a million years contemplate saying to anyone's face," says Dr. Donna Wick, a clinical and developmental psychologist. She notes that this seems to be especially true of girls, who typically don't like to disagree with each other in "real life."

Statistics can back up this trend. Dr. Jean Twenge, an established American psychologist, used data to correlate how the national rise in teen mental health problems mirrors the market penetration of iPhones. Both datasets take an upswing around 2012. These studies show a correlation, not causation, however. It is still worthy to investigate how social media could be affecting teenagers and young adults negatively. A 2017 study of over half a million 8th to 12th graders found that the number exhibiting high levels of depressive symptoms increased by 33% between 2010 and 2015. In the same period, the suicide rate for girls in this age group jumped by 65%.

There was, additionally, a sharp spike in reports of students seeking help at college and university counseling centers, principally for depression and anxiety, with visits jumping 30% between 2010 and 2015. This evidence cannot be taken as conclusive proof that smartphone usage and social media are raising rates of depression in today's youth. There may be other factors at play, but the correlational data certainly warrants a closer look and gives greater credence to investigating youth psychology.

Technology aside, today's youth are generally growing up more slowly, being more likely than previous generations to hang out with their parents, postpone sex, and decline driver's licenses. Dr. Twenge's hypothesizes that this is caused by modern environmental conditions, a theory commonly referred to as a life-history theory. This argues that the speed at which teens "grow up" (which is neither good nor bad) depends on their perceptions of their environment. When the environment is perceived as hostile and competitive, teens take a "fast life strategy," growing up quickly, making larger families earlier, and focusing on survival.

The war is a prime example of this theory; children were forced into factories to cope with a shortage of workers and had to mature into productive members of society at a very young age. A "slow life strategy," in contrast, occurs in times of safer environments where responsibilities, such as work and starting a family, can be postponed to develop greater skills, such as higher education. This phenomenon has been seen to occur across all racial, regional, and classes of youth groups. Thanks to advanced medicine, good quality education standards, and safe societies in much of the western world, a safe environment has been created, resulting in the "slow life strategy" suggested by Twenge's life history theory.

As a knock-on effect, the youth of the 2010s were found to be the "best-behaved generation on record," according to a 511-page report by The Centers for Disease Control. The document from May 2014 reported that teenage pregnancies and their use of drugs and alcohol reached record lows. A 2013 survey showed that the rate of teen smoking dropped to 15.7% (e-cigarette and smokeless tobacco use among teenagers has risen, however) with a teen in 1982 10% more likely to smoke marijuana and 12% more likely to smoke cigarettes than a teen of today. The rate of teenagers having unprotected also sex dropped to 34%, and the rate of teenagers participating in a physical fight dropped to 25%, much lower than their counterparts just 22 years earlier.

Millennials and iGen's are much more tolerant of race and religion than their average predecessors. Women of these younger cohorts represent a larger proportion of the workforce, narrowing the disparities between males and females. Today's young adults are also much better educated than their grandparents, as the share of young adults with a bachelor's degree or higher has steadily climbed since 1968. Among Millennials, around 40% of those aged 25 to 37 have a bachelor's degree or higher, compared with just 15% of the Silent Generation (born 1928 - 1945), roughly a quarter of Baby Boomers and about 30% of Gen-Xers when they were the same age. While educational attainment rates have steadily increased for men and women over the past five decades, the share of millennial women with a bachelor's degree is now higher than that of men – a reversal from the Silent Generation and Boomers. Gen X women were the first to outpace men in terms of education, with a 3-percentage-point advantage over Gen X men in 2001. Before that, late Boomer men in

1989 had a 2-point advantage over Boomer women.

It seems then that the youth of today have been given an unfair bad reputation. Despite claims that millennials are lazy, dependent, and lack the attitude for graft that made boomers great, the statistics couldn't paint a more different story. Today's new generations are the most educated, most tolerant, and hardest working of the lot, with unemployment of under 4% in the U.S. and UK, which are the lowest rates since 1969. Yet environmental conditions, such as expensive housing and stagnant wage growth, are preventing many from obtaining the independence and wealth the boomers accumulated so much easily. No matter how much each generation bickers, one thing is certain: it is inevitable for each generation to complain about their successor.

Conclusion

Each passing year brings its own set of challenges. Whilst life expectancies and the quality of life are increasing in most of the world, thanks to advances in medicine and technology, other issues have hindered progress. A vast number of countries throughout the world were hit by shifting political landscapes throughout the past 10 years. Populism, the idea of "the people" against "the elite," gained traction in both developing and developed countries around the world. Increasing income inequality between the rich and poor, incompetent politicians, constant political bickering, stagnant wages, and high levels of immigration have created the perfect storm for civil unrest. =Combined with media rhetoric and manipulation, this frustration has culminated in the populist movements seen in Great Britain through Brexit, the U.S. through the election of Donald Trump, and various European states such as Italy, Hungary, and Poland.

Donald Trump ushered in a new era of politics for the United States, with his disgust of multilateral partnerships tearing many existing and well-functioning relationships apart. Whilst Trump's brashness has rubbed many world leaders the wrong way, including long-standing allies such as Canada and Mexico, he is the first to stand up to the hegemony that is China in his noble fight against intellectual property theft. Whilst former presidents have been keen to keep the peace, much to more aggressive nations' advantage, Trumps unpredictability can make him a force to be reckoned with. With his finger constantly hovering around the self-destruct button, however, global economic markets are likely to remain jittery.

Europe has, at last, seemed to understand its role as a united global superpower to combat the current unpredictable powers of the U.S., China, and Russia. Spurred by newly elected French President Emmanuel Macron and Germany's Chancellor Angela Merkel, Europe is starting to develop a backbone. The rise of populism and Eurosceptic movements such as Brexit threaten to thwart progress, however. Before Europe can hold its own against the incumbent powers, it first needs to quell nationalist rhetoric caused by stagnant wage growth and mass immigration.

What started as a noble movement to peacefully protest against corrupt and autocratic governments in much of the Middle East and Africa soon turned into mass violence and civil war as incompetent governments attempted to suppress the protests in the only way they knew how – through extreme police brutality and restrictions on freedoms and human rights. Whilst Tunisia provided early encouragement that protests can bring down corrupt incumbents and replace them with a new era of democracy, subsequent attempts by other nations, including Egypt, Libya, and Syria, resulted in horrific state violence and crimes against humanity not seen since the depths of the second world war. Whilst much of the fighting has ceased, the fragile nations are still politically unstable.

America's hold as the most influential superpower has started to wane this past decade as China's aggressive foreign policy and rapid economic growth make it an attractive destination to store wealth. The U.S. dollar's lead as a global currency is also diminishing as the Renminbi and Euro become increasingly attractive to investors seeking to hedge their wealth against the greenback.

Thanks to technological advances, economies are becoming increasingly decentralized as a "sharing economy" emerges. Spare rooms, vehicles, workspaces, and everything in between have become shared commodities between individuals, cutting out the middleman. E-commerce and M-commerce have tightened the reigns on many traditional brick-and-mortar stores, which are closing in droves. The emergence of "virtual stores" through VR technology is expected to increase this effect over the next 10 years.

Despite artificial intelligence making significant progress, the limitations are still very much present. Systematic and repetitive jobs, such as data analysis and factory work, have seen AI seamlessly replace them. Other tasks requiring human traits such as empathy, creativity, and personal skills will be safe for the foreseeable future. Whilst many jobs have been either partially or fully automated, many more have been created as a result of new influxes of technology and the new industries they create. Many of these new jobs and industries, however, require greater intellectual capacity and qualifications, which benefit the new swaths of younger, more educated generations but still leaves those who have been made redundant in peril.

The severity of climate change on the environment has finally moved into the public eye as the frequency and intensity of natural disasters this decade has made it impossible to ignore. Whether it be intense forest fires in rich California or destructive floods in poor Haiti, the public eye is now firm on taking drastic action. We can expect this to become a more influential topic politically and economically this next decade.

Social media has changed how society interacts in both positive and negative ways. Many powerful politicians and businessmen have been unable to hush the scandals that found their way onto social media, including Harvey Weinstein's sexual harassment case and Jeffrey Epstein's child pedophilia ring. Social media has also allowed politically suppressed nations such as Hong Kong and much of the Middle-East to create a voice against their oppressive rulers, offering a hope for change in these corrupt nations. On the other hand, social media and the non-stop break from socializing has led to a worrying trend of depression in young people, whose impressionable minds are easily swayed by false social media "influencers." Social media has also been accused of spreading misinformation and "fake news" as political parties find ways to abuse their influence.

Many psychologists believe pessimism to be an inherently human trait, a defense mechanism to force us to prepare for the worst and improve our chance of survival. It is, therefore, easy to look back at the past decade and remember the worst, with nostalgia leading to unfair comparisons to the "good old days" when life seemed easier. Yet there has never been a better time to be alive than today. Life expectancy is at an all-time high as medical advances significantly improve quality of life and the world is becoming increasingly tolerant of people from all walks of life. Today's youth are the most educated and highest paid and are maturing into adults at a slower pace, not because they are lazy, but because life is safer and the need to develop into an adult is not as pressing; they are able to enjoy more of their youth. Does this not define progress, where future generations surpass preceding ones? To me, that sounds like a good decade. Let's see what the next one brings.